THOUGHTS, MIND POWERS AND FAITH

A CHRISTIAN REFLECTION ON HUMANITY THEORIES

Charlene Ivery-Baba, Ph.D. in Theology

ISBN 978-1-968970-65-9 (Paperback)
ISBN 978-1-968970-66-6 (Ebook)

Inquiries and Book Orders should be addressed to:

Leavitt Peak Press
17901 Pioneer Blvd Ste L #298, Artesia, California 90701
Phone #: 2092191548

ABSTRACT

I researched the theological Christianity approach and a philosophical secular humanitarian idea of humanity to show how their minds can materialize excellent and evil thoughts in our society, where people have the freedom of choice of prevalent behavior to cherry-pick to survive in their lifestyles or choose pleasure. I also proposed that religious and non-religious teachings could influence the human mind for them to process to perform excellent or destructive behaviors. I also focused my attention on Christianity's biblical history to show the sovereignty of God of Christianity is the primary force behind people's acceptable behavior choices. This religion shows a God that entered the world, His presence is here, and He has a plan to separate the good from the evil and return for the good to live with them on earth. The United States, a capitalistic society, is presently challenged with adverse humanitarian teaching to change most Americans' traditional religious lifestyles. The results could be harmful.

Further, I examined the truth behind the faith teaching of Salvation in the Name of Jesus Christ of the Christianity religion compared to the secular education of humanitarian belief. I began my analysis to research the materials because most of humanity believes there is a God. I continued to recognize the God of Christianity as the One True God, as the Supreme Being of all cultures but is worshiped differently. Next, I researched predictors' opinions on how good or bad choices were made and their influence on the human mind. Each one was examined to understand the results of their diagnosis. I proved to support or deny their beliefs or teachings. I ended with discussions on the part of theologians, sociologists, psychologists, and philosophers to understand better why and how humankind's thoughts managed for them to behave this way or not that way. The results ended with their choices of right over wrong or wrong over right, which cannot be denied because the human mind's ideology is created that way.

Keywords: *God, no-God, religion, secular humanism, good and bad thoughts, biblical story, Theology, beliefs, sociology, psychology, Unitarianism, and biblical and systematic theology*

ACKNOWLEDGEMENTS

I give God glory for allowing me to experience the great mystery of His Son Jesus Christ's work on Calvary to grant me the gift of Salvation. Thanks to my significant other Ahmadu, my sisters, my brothers, my family and my community families, and my friends and associates, especially my friend, Mr. Bundy (Herb) forever alive.

I also thank Dr. Mattis, one of my former professors at Grand View University, Bishop West, my longtime friend and forever pastor, and Dr. Jones, who was my Advisor at Atlantic Bible Seminary College. Moreover, thanks to the Saints at Higher Ground Always Abiding Assemblies, those who equip me with biblical knowledge help me continue my Christian journey. They gave me just what I needed to keep me going to stay on task to complete this paper and stay on the Christian journey. Moreover, many thanks to my daughters, Kelly and Lady, and friend Abigail, who God put in my life just at the right time. At the time I needed help to push me along the way to finish and submit this research paper. I give my condolences to my late friend Sadie's family. My heart will always remember her for the many honorable deeds and our forever-lasting friendship, I learned to appreciate.

And great love to my daughter Kelly, who passed away before this book was completed and published.

Thank you all!

Mrs. Charlene Ivery-Baba

CONTENTS

A LOOK INSIDE THIS BOOK

 *"Thoughts, Mind Powers and Faith: A Christian Reflection on Humanity Theories"* is about the human mind: the powerful pushes in the mind that produce good or evil thoughts that make behaviors. It is about God and religions. In addition, the discussions point to the many other causes that influence people's behavior.

People are unique individuals; they can choose to do this or not choose to do that. It is a proven fact that people's physical makeup is made of everlasting thought, such as words that form in their minds, but the body is made of the earth and is not timeless like the words in the mind solid from the thoughts. However, the soul and the spirit are imperishable like words, but the mind supplies the soul, the spirit, and body with concepts of words for humans to make choices. Thus, word choices in the thoughts and behaviors of humankind are eternal because words are blueprints of the human mind.

The mind, the soul, and the spirit of humanity all have divergent functions. The descriptions of each are different too. Their operations are to support the body to be able to interact with each other and to interact with other human beings and all that exists. However, the human mind's primary purpose is to communicate with God, its maker, and keep its self-safe (to reason), to make it possible for humanity to have the right companionship with each other and with God.

The Functions of the Mind, Soul, and Spirit follow:

The <u>human mind</u> is the rational portion of the body, but not the emotional aspects of the intellect; it processes human beings' thoughts, ideas, and desires. The mind is the consciousness of the human body, the memory, and the human brain's imagination that stores all it sees, hears, and feels.

The <u>soul</u> is the non-physical aspect that stores the personal concepts of the divine. The soul longs to have the meaning of life and seeks answers great questions such as, Who am I? Why am I here?

What is my purpose in life, and what is my destiny after life? The soul is eternal and can converse in the languages of creative expressions like art, music, and poetry. The soul, spirit, and body (mind) can access and are accessible to God and Satan's spiritual realms.

The spirit is the vital force of humankind's will, referred to as the spirit of man. Man's spirit is not of the Trinity's Spirit of God; however, man's spirit is an eternal being of God that encourages good choices. The spirit of humanity provides the body with the ability to function on its own. He is humanity's life force enabling them to communicate with God, Satan, and all existence. His title is developer or motivator that pushes humanity's ideas into action.

WHAT ABOUT THIS BOOK

People of faith ask questions, what does it mean to be religious? There are so many religions and philosophies, which make it hard to choose the right one, even if that is possible. Thus, selecting the right religion takes a person to perform research and obtain knowledge to determine what it means to be a genuinely religious person and what faith in God through religion means.

There are three parts of this book, to help enlighten your thoughts about understanding religion and spiritual faith. The book examined humankind's minds and choices made under different influences or choices and without being influenced. As human beings, we are influenced to make choices that might be right or might be wrong that can be helpful in some ways or harmful in others. This book aims to see how the mine materialized and the pushing factors that assist our decision-making.

The book's first part introduces man, revealing how humanity thinks in seven biblical dispensation periods arranged by God. They start at the beginning of time and end with the judgment of life of human beings. Thus, living eternally in heaven or hell is based on religion or faith guidelines and how they choose to believe and live according to that faith.

The second part is about the God of the Holy Bible and examined Christianity. The in-depth examination of faith teachings to investigate the effects it has on people believing in God, the Salvation differences in other religions, faith, and the moral codes of ethics. The object of studying the Bible is to find the signature of the One True Spiritual God.

The third part of the book goes through most religions of the world. The outlook is for you to see how all religions instill faith teaching and the moral code of living. The perspective is to see how the One True God plays a part in each religion and faith teaching. The object of perusing is to see the God of the Holy Bible in all religions.

In conclusion, the discussion looked at various human resemblances of humanity's acts when deciding on a particular subject. The discussions of experts on authors who had written multiple topics and books. The approach gave an insight into how the mind behaves this way and not that way. The issues were in line with the choices of humankind's behavior and the outcome it might incur if influenced or not influenced.

Some parts of the book ended with the final remarks, but some did not have them. The book ended with a conclusion that gave insight into the choices and the predictions. Each prediction was the perception of choosing evil over good. The two terminologies examined were to understand why humanity chooses hell over heaven, even though the outcomes are eternal in both ways. One offers joy and peace, while the other offers suffering and pain, which is the final choice of humanity.

INTRODUCTION

 MAN IN THE WORLD

The Holy Bible

Next the theory of the Holy Bible, this Introduction centered on humanity's life as they go through the eras of dispensations arranged by God. The eras of dispensations are the biblical time zones that God governs according to His Law and His gift of Salvation to those named. The covenant agreements are in harmony with the Law and Salvation of God. The covenant displays God's Law and Salvation arrangements. They outline the results of humanity when they honor or dishonor the treaties of the covenant. It is humanity's responsibility to fulfill the covenant agreement to live a life free from sin. The grace of God displays his mercy, love, and power to forgive if they break the covenant pacts. In each Dispensation, the Law of God points to the grace of God that forgives sin. *There are seven dispensations in biblical history.*

The "seven dispensations" [1] of the biblical time zones run consecutively. The first is the Dispensation of Innocence (Gen. 1:3-3:6). In this dispensational era, the Law of God said, "do not eat from the tree of the knowledge of good and evil; if they do, they will die. The Law of God said they should not do it, but they did, and the grace of God made a sacrifice to cover their sin of disobedience.

In the second Dispensation of Conscience (Gen. 3:7-8:14). The Law of God ran alongside God's Salvation that encouraging humanity to do good. Humankind's conscience of sin rejected God's offer of Salvation. Their conduct was evaluated in their choice of evil over good. All who lived in the land-practiced evil, but Noah, a righteous man, choose to obey God. Because of his righteousness and obedience, God asked him to build an ark. His family and certain animals entered the ark to bypass the flood, allowing God's grace to save a portion of humanity.

In the third Dispensation of Civil Government (Gen. 8:15-11). During this time, people forgot about God's Salvation, became obsessed with selves, and decided to build a tower to reach heaven. They disobeyed the command of God to scatter throughout the earth. This happens after the flood; Noah showed disrespect toward God when he became drunk and revealed, that he was incapable of ruling the land. The grace of God confused each one's languages (instead of his judgment), and they safely left from building the towel to fulfill God's command to scatter across the face of the earth.

In the fourth Dispensation of Patriarchal Rule or Dispensation of Promise (Gen. 11:10-Exodus 18:27). Abraham had faith to believe in God. God's Salvation revealed to Abraham that if he and his offspring served Him, He (God) would be their God. God commanded Abraham to offer his son as a sacrifice. Abraham became the father of the faith because he believed God. God substituted another sacrifice when Abraham went to the top of the hill to sacrifice his son. God had a goat for Abraham to offer instead of his son.

The fifth Dispensation revealed the <u>Mosaic Law</u>. (Exodus 19:1-John 14:30). Moses received the Law of God directly from the hands of God. However, when he left speaking with God and went down from the mountain to find the children of Israel, worshiping an idol. They had built a golden calf to worship. They had rejected the Salvation of God repeatedly until God told them they could not enter the promised land, Moses too because he strike the rock God said speak to. Their children went to enter the promised land instead of them.

Finally, humanity entered the <u>Dispensation of Grace</u> (Acts 2:1-Rev. 19:21). During the era of grace, the Salvation of God came in the Name of Jesus Christ. Through Jesus, humanity's sins are forgiven and not judged according to the Law of God; instead, God sealed them as children of God. Only if they confess their sins against God and believe that Jesus Christ is the Son of God that paid the price to redeemed them from the power of the adversary. Jesus was born of a woman who conceived him through the Holy Spirit. He lived in a human body without sin; He died on the cross and rose from death to sit at the right hand of God. All power and authority are in his hands. He will return to establish the Kingdom of God on earth one day hopefully soon.

In the <u>Millennium Dispensation</u> (Revelation 20:1-15). The Law of God laid down guidelines for humanity to follow Jesus Christ as their ruling king. Satan is bound for a thousand years. God commands people to be obedient and obey Jesus' authority as he rules the world's affairs. At the end of the thousand years, Satan will be released, and rebels will formulate an attempt to overthrow Jesus' seat of authority, but they will fail. Satan and these rebels are going to be thrown into the everlasting fire of hell.

Summary

The seven dispensations were displayed to see how God worked in history and what the outcome entailed. God's plan of Salvation offered to people throughout history has always been their responsibility to reason to understand the significance of the offer. Sin is a biblical terminology that means actions against the will of God. Sin and evil are words used interchangeably in the Bible as Satan's powers that influence people to disobey God. It is evident that humankind's actions are either good or bad, and the reality of their mental powers is programmed for them to function based on good or bad decisions and choices.

Righteousness is a concept of God. God is a righteous God, and all His Words He speaks are righteous too. The Salvation of God safeguards humanity from the works of Satan. People do not have the power to withstand Satan alone and need the power of God to subdue Satan's words. Within the Salvation of God are Words of God that will defeat Satan. This section has discussed the influences on the human mind in the eras of dispensation. Evil powers motivate people to misbehave and do evil acts. The Holy Spirit's power administers God's gift of Salvation, empowering humanity to do righteous and good actions.

THE GOD OF THE HOLY BIBLE

 ### God of Religion

To understand the reality of God, an explanation needs to be confirmed, just who is God and what makes him God. Most religions teach they serve the one true God, especially Christianity, Judaism, and Islam. They believe He is the creator of all things. He is the ultimate powerful force of nature and life. The eternal image of God's presence starts from the beginning and is never-ending. The One True, such as Yahweh (and other names), because of His definition, characteristics, and personages, say He is God.

This section aims to see *what makes God - God*. As the supreme being, the characteristic of God must be omnipotent, omnipresent, and omniscient. His power, beauty, and sovereignty displayed throughout the earth and the universe reveal who He is. He is the Father of humanity, the fighter against evil, and the life-sustainer of all existence, including nature. The definition of God makes it easy for every human being to recognize God. His descriptions, character, and personages reveal who is God. He and only He is God.

The titles of God are paramount above all others. They are the design of His characters. The Highest God (El `Elyon) is an amazing title because it is given only to Him. He sits high in His seat of authority and rules the entire universe. God as the Almighty God ('El Shaddai) is colossal to all others. No other can create the universe, earth, people, and all existence other than Him. The God that said I AM THAT I AM statement means, "It is what it is," and no one can change it. God is all these titles and more. He is the only Supreme Being that everyone calls God. He is the Lord who honors and sanctifies. Yahweh - (Jehovah) M' Kaddish, allowing humanity to come close to worship.

Definition: God's nature is the one creator, sustainer of life, and the universe and natural maintainer. He is God because of his supreme natural ability to do things that no other or anything else can do. There is no explanation of who He is, only what He has done. The meaning of God is according to every act that He has performed throughout history. Finally, the description of God is indescribable because no one has seen Him in person.

Characteristics: God's attribute of love is active in human feelings. Agape love tops all other love. It shows the love of God not according to the love of man, but the love of God that is the root of goodness. Agape is the highest form of love. Agape love is a supreme and excellent type of love that is unconditional love. This love in humans will obey every Word that proceeds out of the mouth of God.

His Personages: The Trinity reveals the personages of God. The three forms of God are the Father, the sustainer of lives, the Son who creates life, and the Holy Spirit who empowers life into existence.

They are separate in identity, but they are one in substance. Any one of the Trinity will not work without the other, but each has its own identity and purposes.

What Makes God the One True God?

God is the Supreme Being that created humanity. He created all things. God's characteristics make him God all-powerful, ever-present-knows all and see all. Without these capabilities, God could not be God, and He could not have the ability to rule and maintain His creation.

First, the omnipotent characteristic proves He is of great power. As the supreme being, He can do just what He says He will, like maintaining the powerful forces of nature are examples of His power. The God of omnipotent is infinite or limitless because His Word affirms His actions is one of a kind because of His creative abilities. His Word is incapable of replacement with another. The Word of God is part of the personage of the three (Trinity).

Second, God is omnipresent, allowing His presence to be everywhere because He is Spirit. His universal ability causes Him to be always present, at the beginning of time and at the end of time. The biblical God of history acts throughout time. He is the Infinite Spirit of the universe. The universal Name of God works in all religions. His actions shown in nature are an example of His powerful force behind his Name. The Words of God represent his very presence, of the ideal of God in the minds of humanity.

Third, God has the characteristic of omniscience, an all-knowing God. God knows all in the lives of people because He created them. God's knowledge about them gives Him the edge to predict their future, see their need, and understand and know the outcome of their choices in life. He has the knowledge and ability to maintain the world and take care of its inhabitants at any time. His all-knowing capabilities create His personages of the Trinity. God always sits on the high seat of His authority. He rules as God in the capacity of the Father, the Son, and the Holy Spirit. God's Kingdom is spiritual and has the power to rule in heaven as well on the physical earth.

The Argument of the One True God

The argument of the One True God is about the only God, which is possible because humanity internally knows specific characteristic that identifies Him. Even their signature displays His presence in the reality of their existence. God is the God of many nations or cultures. The concept of God developed according to the interaction of the settings. For example, many cultures worship many gods, but God is one, in three persons: the Father, Son, and Holy Spirit. They share the same nature and essence, but their jobs are different One reason God must always be The Father, is He reigns high in heaven, forever as the Supreme Power who maintains what He made.

 ## GOD in MAN

Jesus the Anointed Messiah

The Virgin Mary gave birth to Jesus, affirming that he is the Messiah sent by God. His miraculous birth equipped him for his ministry to bring the Old Testament promise of Salvation to the world. Jesus is the Son of God ordained to act in the capacity of God to redeem the world back from under Satan's rule to be ruled under the authority of God. Jesus sent back the gift of Salvation when he returned to his Father from the dead. The gift of Salvation empowers humanity to obey God's covenant agreements for their protection from Satan their adversary and empowers them to live an absentee life of sin. God's gift of Salvation guarantees humanity to live a good life, but only if they follow the plan of Salvation. First, Jesus came to teach humanity how to honor God. He offered himself as a sacrifice to dismantle Satan's rule over the souls of humanity, making them not acceptable to sin anymore.

Jesus' Name is the authority of God on earth. Scripture proclaims, "And there is salvation in no one else, for there is no other name under heaven given among men by which they are saved from a sinful life." His identity is part of the Trinity of God in His Son's likeness and is God's Word. The scriptures teach the sole purpose of Jesus coming into the world is to redeem the offspring of Abraham and open the door for the gentiles to accept him as their personal Lord and Savior so they can gain access to the Salvation of God. Cited from Acts 4:12 [A2]

God in Jesus as Man

Jesus' title Emmanuel means God dwells with humanity. God in man came in the Name of Jesus to save humanity from sin. Jesus performed this service to manifest the presence of God's participation in his ministry. Jesus, as Emmanuel revealed to humanity; who God is; his power, and what they will become if they abide in God's Salvation. God's Salvation opened the door and gave humanity permission to live now in the Kingdom of God on earth (Kingdom of Heaven).

The title Emmanuel acts in other capacities too. First, as Emmanuel, he is a Rabbi, the Supreme Teacher of God who taught with God's authority. Emmanuel, the Savior of God, causes humanity to experience the presence and calling of God. Third, as Emmanuel, the Compassionate one from God, humanity witness God as the living reality of the compassions of love he shows while on earth. In addition, as Emmanuel the Judge, they possess the Spirit of God to resolve their inner conflict of good and evil.

The Messages of God in Jesus

From the Old Testament to the New and from dispensations to dispensations, God's message to humanity has always been the same to repent to bear fruit worthy of it because God's Kingdom is nearby. The battle of conflict of choice is the way of life for humanity. The reality for them to survive competes with their truth to depend on God to supply their every need is a great struggle. This has always been a dilemma in the minds of humanity throughout time.

Jesus came to show humanity how the fruits of darkness manifested in their lives through temptations. There are three influences that humanity should be aware of that could make significant differences in their choices over evil. First, Jesus showed them they struggle with the power of deception to believe they need immediate gratification. For example, physical hunger for food or desires they deem more important than obeying God's Word. Second, their dilemmas over saving their lives because of their feeling of the danger of not having enough or of being poor will stop their way of a successful life . All they must do is receive the Salvation of God, and they will live safe under God's protection. Third, they struggle between two choices, to choose to live under the Word of God in His kingdom or decide to live under Satan's words in his kingdom. First, Jesus met all temptations with fasting to lessen the power of the flesh, and then He used the Word of God to defeat the yearnings of the sins of Satan's temptations, defeating ever sinful acts of Satan.

Passions of God in Jesus

God's passion offers His only Son as a sacrificial sacrifice to equip humanity with the power of God's Salvation. The Son of God came into this world to die, to go down to hell to win the battle over desires of the flesh and the sting of death. He rose from death, came back to the earth, and went to heaven to be with His Father again. Jesus won the war, allowing God to send the Holy Ghost to indwell in people to empower them to live according to the Laws of God under the power of the gift of Salvation.

The passion of Jesus He went through disrespect and disbelieve of the people He came to redeem. He went through horrific suffering, a horrifying execution, and excruciating pain to die hanging from across as a gift offering of His Father to win the battle over the power of evil over humanity.

Important Teachings of Jesus

In most cases, Jesus spoke in parables. The parables Jesus said gave insights into His messages. His parables spark spiritual sense in some people, but they also served to make them aware of the dark spirituality in others. Jesus said He spoke in parables because "seeing they do not see and hearing they do not hear, nor do they understand." The Words of Jesus turned up as a light in humanity's hearts, but the light revealed the dark souls in others. He came to bring truth, Salvation, and grace to those who sought after the righteousness of God. Cited from Mark Chapter 13 [A2]

THE HOLY SPIRIT

The Gift of God

Now the earth was formless and empty, darkness was over the surface of the deep, and the Spirit of God hovered over the waters. God said, "Let there be light," and it acted. The Holy Spirit first hovered over the waters to gather information and to get things ready for God to speak His word into existence. If so, then the Holy Spirit's position is to get things ready, and God speaks to them into reality for the Word to perform. For example, he makes the change or transformation of a person from carnality to spirituality; that person at first had no idea how to love, glorify, and obey God, but after he or she is vested with the Holy Spirit, a change occurred. Now that person speaks the Salvation of God with power and joy into reality. Cited from Genesis 1:3 [A2]

The Holy Spirit Lives as the Love of God in Humanity

In the Old Testament, the Holy Spirit came upon people for special services; but in the New Testament, Jesus requested God to send Him to abode within the believers. The Holy Spirit seals believers with the seal of God. The gift of Salvation is the love of God, a gift that is so wonderful and perfect. The gift of Salvation is so perfect that it is impossible for humanity not to exercise God's behavioral commands excellently. Still, if not, they have neglected the ideal life-changing grace of the Salvation of God.

The two attributes of the Holy Spirit to perfect sinners are love and joy. They are God's attributes that the Holy Ghost prepares believers for service. Love is, above all feelings, considered the cause of the highest obedience to God. God's love is different from humanities in that it represents agape love. Agape love is spiritual and understands the first Law of the commandments to be obedient to God's will, which is the first and utmost necessity of absentee of the relationship with sin. In II Corinthians, Chapter 13 tells the story of God's love.

The joy of the Holy Spirit is a motivator. His joy represents things that will take place in the future. The Holy Spirit evokes emotions of well-being in humans. He shows them their earnest possessions of the things to come, and they see the power of God transform their lives. They possess the eternal state of true happiness as a part of the family of God. His source of joy gives bliss and delight in their adverse experiences on earth. The believers rejoice and are glad in the wilderness journey with joy and hope to one day to abide in the Kingdom of God when it comes to abiding on the earth.

Second Corinthians Chapter 13, Paul declared that the Holy Spirit came bearing and giving out many spiritual gifts from God. He solely expressed that believers must understand the importance of their connection with the gift and their responsibility to discipline themselves. First, the gifts are God's to use accordingly. If they are misused, there is a harsh penalty to pay. Jesus spoke about the misuse of the Holy Spirit. He said, "Therefore I tell you, every sin and blasphemy will be forgiven men, but the blasphemy against the Holy Spirit shall not be forgiven." Cited from Matthew 12:31 [A2]

In addition, human beings are irrational, and their uncontrollable desires to encounter sin are without question. The warfare of humanity against the urges to sin is the dilemma within the human body and their eyesight's wishes to fulfill. The fruits of God's love are the most outstanding defense of humanity against their acts of sin.

The Bible proclaims that there are many powers of God, such as love, joy, peace, and longsuffering, and there are more.

The Acts of the Holy Spirit

When a person repents and confesses that Jesus is their personal Lord and Savior, the Holy Spirit's first act is to seal that believer with the seal of God as a member of the family of God. The three reasons God fills believers with the Spirit of God are, the first is to prepare or enlighten them for God's services. The second reason the Holy Spirit empowers them with the knowledge and wisdom of God, is to know, understand, and participate in the work of God, believers must possess the knowledge of God. Next, the skill is given but learning how to use it takes patience and practice. The last act of the Holy Spirit is getting believers ready to become servants and workers of God. The bearer of the gifts is the Holy Spirit. He is the delivery service, not the individual, which is why believers must treat their bodies as living sacrifices, holy, and acceptable sacrifices to be able to do the services of God, which is their reasonable service.

The Holy Ghost, counselor who councils in a beautiful and gentile Spirit. The gentile and quiet Word of the Holy Spirit gives believers a taste of things to come. He guides and protects the believers in spiritual battles. He is the Spirit of Truth. His job helps humanity in their weakness, empowering them with the Word of God for services. He sanctifies and equips believers under the decrees of God's Salvation. This is the work of the Holy Spirits.

Great is the mystery of godliness. The Holy Spirit empowers the Church to live transcendent lifestyles. He is the enabler of the spiritual things of God. His language is pure energy. He is the power behind the Word of God. He makes things happen. He is not a part of material identity but a member of God and a part of the holy elite spiritual army.

He embodies believers with the power to win the war on Satan and his demons. He knows about all the things of God. The battles are not believers to fight, but the battle is the Lord who will win the fight every time. The principles of God are what determine the Holy

Spirit's actions or his functions. He takes from the spiritual realm and manifests them into the material world to show the works of God.

THE CHURCH IN THE WORLD

The Mission of the Church

The Church is a chosen race, a royal priesthood, and a holy nation; God chose the Church as his people to declare the beautiful deeds of Jesus Christ and show his love to the world. Jesus called the Church out of darkness into the marvelous light of God's Salvation. They declare and live the excellency of God's beautiful gift when they go into the world and speak about the good news of the gospel.

On the cross, Jesus Christ died to offer his sacrificial blood is the deal paid to end Satan's contract to rule over humanity's nature. Satan is the Prince of the Air and rules all the kingdoms on earth through humankind's minds. Jesus paid the price with his blood to bring the Kingdom of Heaven on earth. The Church is the separated human race that God called out of the world.

The church is a physical place also called the Saints. Saints gather there to glorify God and learn about the Laws of God and his gift of Salvation. The Church becomes the body of Christ when they perform rites that remind them of the sacrifice Jesus did on the Cross of Calvary. The Church is where the saints of God fellowship, experience God's spiritual insight, and see the mighty works of God. In the Church, believers learn, receive, and earn to bear the marks of Jesus Christ.

The atonement of Jesus Christ released the entire world from under the rule of Satan. They are no longer obligated to obey the commands of Satan and live in his kingdoms. The Salvation agreement is the contract God established for humanity to have the ability to live under the decrees empowered by His gift of Salvation under the power of the Holy Spirit. The covenant language states what the grace of God, Jesus, and the Holy Spirit will do for the Church, the

Hebrews, and the world, their rewards for keeping them, and the outcomes if broken.

The contents of the covenant agreements are the promises of the Salvation of God. The promise of God starts in Genesis and ends in the book of Revelation. In the Dispensation of Grace, all of God's promises to the Church, He answers with a yes. God's promises entail God's Laws designed of His grace to ask the Church to live by faith, believe as they obey His commands, and live by the covenant agreements to have Salvation power.

God's promises have always been His plan to answer peoples' requests to get them out from under the bondage of Satan's sins. He attempted to answer their appeal in the Old Testament, leading Israel out of bondage, through the wilderness, into the promised land, but they forfeited the covenant agreement. In the New Testament, Jesus brought humanity out of bondage, offering His blood as a sacrifice, and then he went to heaven and sent back the Holy Spirit who abides in the believers. Jesus Christ's response to the Church as the Church is response to Him. He says, ask and it shall be given to you.

Jesus is the head of the Church. The Church belongs to Him, and they cannot exist without him. The Church is the body of Christ, and he being the head completes the Church's fullness. The Church sits with Christ in heavenly places, for through him, they have access by one Spirit (Holy Spirit) unto the Father. The Church experiences the glory and majestic power of Christ only because she is the body of Christ, and he is the head. The fullness of the Church's deity is because they allow the Spirit of Christ to dwell within them and obey His requests. The Church is God's workmanship He created in Christ Jesus for good works.

The Responsibilities of the Holy Spirit to the Church

The Holy Spirit is the earnest of the Church's inheritance. He is the Spirit of God given to believers. When believers accept the Holy Spirit's gift of Salvation, they are sealed and marked inwardly as ones consecrated to God for good works. The Holy Spirit is the gift of God, a token to the Church. The Holy Spirit gives the Church authority to participate in the fullness of the divine blessing. He is the Church's guide, the teacher, and the counselor of the things of God, now, and things to come.

The Church's Responsibilities of Covenant Agreements

In Christianity, Salvation (also called deliverance or redemption) is Christ saving humanity from their sins and Satan's power over their lives. The consequence of sin is death and separation from God. Through Christ's death and resurrection, humanity experiences redemption from sin and justification to receive God's gift of Salvation.

The responsibilities of the Church come in two manifestations of services, inside the Church and outside. Inside the Church, the believers participate in worship services and sacraments, but out of it, they live worthy to be the children of God, and they are to complete the request of Jesus to tell the world about the good news of Salvation.

In the book of Revelation, Chapters 2-3, Jesus addressed seven churches. His statements of authority told the churches that they needed to do something to get some things right. He warned them of things they still needed to change. The addresses of Jesus to the Churches then are immensely helpful warnings to the Churches today.

To the Church of Ephesus, Jesus said, "Return to your first love or first works." To the Church of Smyrna, He said, "Stay faithful until death." To the Church of Pergamos, He affirmed, "get rid of Balaam and Nicolaitans' doctrines." To the Church of Thyatira, He declared, "get rid of Jezebel, who calls herself a prophetess." To the Church of Sardis, He said, "Your works are dead; be watchful and strengthen what you have." To the Church of Philadelphia, Jesus said, "because of your works, a door is opened, and you will be kept from the hour of temptation." Cited from Chapters 2-3 in Revelation [A2]

THE OPPONENT OF GOD

 ## The Work of the Devil

Christianity presents Satan as a former Archangel of God. He held the position of Minister of Music in heaven. Satan, in an arrogant tone, said I could rule heaven in place of God. He recruited an army of angels, and they fought against the army of God. The Archangel Michael, leader of the Army of God, won the battle. He threw Satan and His demons (former angles) out of heaven, and they landed on earth. The Bible declared, "Woe to you, O earth and sea, for the devil has come down unto you in great wrath because he knows that his time is short." Cited from Revelation 12:12 [A2].

He rules the earth under the title of the Prince of the Air. He possesses and uses powers opposite to God's Words. His influence was resolved by Jesus, the Word of God. The Word of God came to earth as a man; he died and came back from the dead with the keys of heaven and hell. He has the power to rule actions in heaven, on earth, and in hell. Jesus stopped Satan's rule over humanity's souls, to take their souls to hell to live in total evilness for eternity. Hell is a place God prepared for Satan and His demons to live, but because of humanity's sinful nature, their destiny is hell as well. The life, death, and resurrection of Jesus paid the price to release humanity's minds and souls from under Satan's rule. Now humanity has the power to receive and use the good promises of God.

Powers of War over the Thoughts of Humanity

The tedious task of humanity is trying to do good over evil in their minds and lives. Even so, it is their responsibility to separate, choose, and justify the use of God's powers over the powers of Satan. Throughout the Bible, good and evil forces are seen performing good or evil acts in humanity's lives. Biblical history tells of the wars over the entitlement of the minds and souls of humankind. The thoughts and souls of humanity have extraordinary significance to God and

Satan. The picture the Bible shows, God has a great desire to preserve human life and its societies; but Satan's greatest desire is for them to destroy themselves. Humanity must understand the reasons behind their choices of words and behaviors.

Humanity was created to live under God's Laws, a life-of-hope pleasing to the creator, but they rebelled. Humankind is assessed continuously under God's powers of good and the opposite powers of God's Word. In life, they have confessed their belief in the opposite Words of God, which shows their confidence in believing and experiencing depravity in the face of powerless living. Their wrong choice or their desires take them out of the will of God's plan of salvation for them.

People can choose to live a life under God's power to protect them to live a good life and enjoy the fruits of Gods. Under God's power of Salvation, they are empowered with the seal of God's Holy Spirit to live good and righteous lives. The first people forfeited humankind's stay in the garden of Eden's original economy of God. Today people could live in the spiritual Kingdom of Heaven, another perfect economy of God. They are empowered with the power of the Spirit of God to resist Satan. Their minds are transformed to be like Christ when their minds focus on Christ's words.

Satan and Sin

God's judgment in history happened because of evil influences, which caused God's created order to be compromised. The Devil masked his deceptive words to deceive the first woman and man. His remarks were desirable, but his whole purpose was to get them to sin against God. Satan and his demons are the cosmic powers of evil and disorder. When humanity chooses to live an obedient life to Christ, they experience the ability to honor God and put Him as the ruler of their minds and heart. Only then will they have a power greater than Satan's power over their destructive lives.

God's promises to humanity were signed as effective powers at the beginning of time, and they will stay in effect until the end times. He said, "if you disobey me, you will surely die. (Gen. 3:1-2) Satan still uses the same tactics he used at the beginning of time. He starts with convening humanity to reason against their obedience to God. Satan also influences society to question the authority of God. For example, in the Garden of Eden, he told the woman to eat the fruit from the tree of knowledge of good and evil, and she will become wise like God knowing good and evil. He did not tell them there are consequences if you know good and evil.

In addition, the devil still utilizes humanity's curiosity to get them to question the commands of God. His three tactics are first; he used temptation to satisfy the hunger they think needs immediate gratification. Next, Satan uses the allure of worship of idols to make humans believe they are more important than worshiping God. Then he also uses the opposite of the Words of God to contradict God's Words.

Destiny of Humanity after Death

Many people believe there are three ways to live after death. Some say their exit ticket after life is to go to heaven, while others say hell is not real and why would God put me in hell. Still, others say they live in heaven and hell now on earth, and others do not believe in either. The perception of life after death is a concept in humanity's minds, and it cannot be determined only if they chose not to accept where they are destined to go as they live. Going to heaven or hell are promises of God. All of God's promises are true.

PART II

 RELIGIONS AND PHILOSOPHIES

The God of Worship

Religions and philosophies are the products of the thoughts of people. One person believes but another does not. It is their belief to determine if a religion's focus is to worship God. One way to define how God is glorified is the definition of what God should entail. This section aims to determine which religion, or philosophy fits the criteria of how to worship God.

God is a supernatural spirit being. He is not a reality of the existence of things on earth. He only materializes in the thoughts of humanity. He is God because of his titles and power to perform what no human or being can produce. He is God of all humanity's thoughts, all they see, all they feel, and all they image into existence. Even so, how they use them is a different story.

Definition of Religion

The definition of religion is a system of beliefs, practices, and worship of a deity or deities. However, the many approaches to worship must play forward to determine what the deity or deities worshiped, and how the participants are treated, all decide the definition of religion. There are thousands of ways to practice beliefs. Many religious practices are in line with the governments' ruling authorities, or the methods are features of their cultures. Still, people have encountered great spiritual teachers that have enlightened minds to accept their religious visions. However, religions' infallibility must meet the precise, perfect, and adequate design of standards to honor, obey, and worship God.

The Idea of Worship

Religions teach people to honor, worship, and depend on a Supreme Deity. The inner knowledge of humanity does not coincide with its surroundings. Therefore, humanity's thoughts formed the concept of a Supreme Being who can resolve all their worries and problems that are impossible for them to change. The human mind functions in a paradox of beliefs and disbeliefs. Humanity's curiosity and need are based on their ideas—for example, the best gift given to God and the impression the return will be the best. The foundation of human trust sits on a solid foundation of exchange, but the theory of return of worship misses God's identity. The reason for worshiping God, which should be precise, perfect, and adequate worship of God's design to be worship, and their return, should be the same.

Humanity's Reasons for Worship

History gives gray areas in how humanity worshiped God compared to whom, what, and how they worshiped Him today. To honor means devotion or recognition to deities, mostly to God, but worship can mean worshiping any objects deemed superior to oneself. Yesterday humanity worshiped the moon and stars, animals, nature, and many gods. Although humanity appears civil in the way they worship God today, there is still evidence showing they still miss true worship of God in the same methods as yesterday.

Today's Worshipers

In most cases, the image of God is to worship, and His attributes are feared. Still, certain religions worship objects other than God. Their worship may take a different approach stating the worship is directed to the One True God; even so, the worship executed another kind of deity that does not match the signature of the True Spirit God.

Worshippers of Animals

Yesterday, On a Japanese Island, archaeologists found evidence of a bear called "Kamui." [2] Kamui means gods. Today, in one of the sects of Hinduism, monkeys are worshiped as a deity. Hanuman, the monkey, is a reincarnation of Shiva, the God of destruction. Today scientists in the United States of America deemed human's biological makeup evolved from monkeys.

Worshippers of the Stars and the Moon

Today, the most common worshipper of celestial objects is the practice called "Astrometry." [3] They worship the stars and other heavenly bodies as deities. The polytheistic system is the most common instance of worshippers of the sun gods and moon gods. Yesterday,

Babylonians and Greco-Romans worshipped Mercury, Venus, Mars, Jupiter, and Saturn as deities. These deities showed uncontrollable, unknowable, and destructible powers, like nature. The worship description does not fit the true meaning to worship God; therefore, they are not honoring the One True Spirit God but see His attributes to be worship.

Worshippers of Nature

Today, the worshippers of nature call themselves "Pantheism." [4] They worship the earth, not the prescriptions of the meaning of God. Today, Pantheism mimics' yesterday in Greek worshippers, who worshiped the Greek earth goddess, Gaia. Back then, the reason for worshiping Gaia was a belief that life and the planet co-evolved together. When they adore her, she used her power to keep life's habitation in constant relationship with the earth, eliminating any dreadful thing that could cause life not to thrive.

PART III

 EXPERTS DISCUSS THE IMPACT OF THE HUMAN MIND

Influences on the Human Mind

The inquiries about each subject of the discussions gave insight into the type of questions asked. The methods of probes used were to evoke the reasons behind the arguments. The inquiries lessen the tension between the two different subjects. One or two examinations of the subject performed and answered were to start the discussions.

Below are the selections of inquiries.

Inquiries

The investigation searched through many references to understand the subject manner. The questions used gave an insight into the challenges in the discussion. They challenge people to see the difference in the way they worship and serve God and see the significance in their lives because they believe in him. The research continued the inquiry about living a secular life as opposed to a religious one. Questions asked what benefits are rewarded for living a spiritual lifestyle in comparison to living a secular lifestyle.

The example proposed inquiry is about the Church of the Twenty Century. Questions were given and asked to lead up to one discussion. The queries used biblical reasoning to dispute secular ideas of doing good and no harm to determine which one produced the best action in societal living. The inquiry questions centered on whether the Church should show tolerance to other religions or religious philosophers. They believe in no absolutes.

Inquiry Questions

Does Unitarianism worship God?

1. What is the definition of Unitarianism, and is it the same as a religion?
    "Unitarianism believes in the toleration of others," no one can grasp the whole so all lifestyles should be embraced with love and no harm. They do not believe in Trinity. (Johnston (2007) They promote each person should have the opportunity to live their philosophy of life. This idea is not in the scriptures of the Bible. "Let this mind be in you which was also in Christ Jesus. (Philippians 2:5)

1. Denying existence in creation, they reject the creative work of God. Genesis chapter 1 started, "In the beginning, God created the heavens and the earth."
2. They disregard the Bible as the Word of God and deny its executive commands of God. They believe in the theory of revolution. Jesus said in Matthew 24:35, heaven and earth will pass away, but my words by no means will pass away. Timothy 3:16, "We must honor the Bible because it is the inerrant, eternal, and truthful Word of God.

Discussion Question of Theologian

Is Unitarianism compatible with Christianity?

Scriptures say no because it lacks the teachings of Christianity. Christians follow specific commands and covenants to know and obey God and receive God's promises. The Law of God commands Christians to act this way, and if an agreement of salvation is forfeited, the correction they seek the solution from the scripture. Christians believe and accept the commands of God without reservation.

Unitarianism falls under secular humanism. They believe in the same format of reasons. Nevertheless, they say no to the design of biblical religion to change or take away the concept. The establishment of religion is for a specific purpose, and that is to worship, respect, and honor God as the Supreme Spiritual Being. He is our Father, and He knows best.

The drawbacks of secularism are that it has inadequacies. They are, it provides a partial and distorted evaluation of human personality. It does not offer humanity a redeeming feature to seek in times of problem and hold to a final hope. The authority proposes tentative forum judgments, not providing society with the assurance of certainty. The offer is temporal and does not offer an "investment for life." [6] Secularism is a spiritual community that humanity finds fellowship. It does not see the Spirit of God as a reality.

Christianity views the worship of God foremost. God gives life, the judge of all existence because He is the creator of all. In the Name of Jesus is Christians' authority. His Name is God's powerhouse in the heavenly kingdom community here on earth. The Holy Spirit, humanity's comforter, counselor, and companion through Him is the avenue they take to communicate through Jesus to God. The way of life for Christian is allowing the Holy Spirit to direct them and protect them then they are empowered and capable of following God's Law to lead them into immortality.

The story behind Christianity is the given fact that humanity could evaluate themselves and determine what is right and what is wrong. The Law of God laid down rules for society could see the wrongs in their lives. Secularism does not provide an outlet for humankind to consider the various dimensions of life to deem rights and wrongs. The outlook of life for them is to suppose humanity as the ultimate "supremacy of man." "The Protagoras dictum," Man is the measure of all things," has been in the secularist's gospel" [6] for centuries.

 **CONCLUSION** SUMMARY OVERVIEW   The introduction went through biblical history concerning humanity's responsibilities to God. In each Dispensation, society had agreements to follow to live in the economy of God, but in most cases, they did not agree with his commands. The outlook for humanity to enter living in a safe environment is their agreement. Heaven is not reserved for a select few. It is open to everyone who will put his or her trust in Jesus. The greatest promise God gave to the world when He said, "For God so loved the world that He gave His only begotten Son that whosoever believe in Him shall not perish but will have eternal life. Cited by John 3:16. [A2]

The dilemma that follows humanity: They ask if it is worth living a godlike life, or if the odds do not add up. For it is better to live a life of pleasure and honor one's desires. Is it true we should live life to be happy and gain what we want in life and define its effects as the only things God wants us to have? Happiness is the first and most goal to reach in life. If one should live for God or live for self, the two are at odds.

The second part examined problems with religion, philosophies, and no religions as they honor or dishonor God. How do they differ if one says it is from God, and another says it is of man? They are hard to differ from each other. The only rule to follow is good vs. evil, but what is right and what is wrong. We know that harm is malicious and giving good gifts is good, but how do we determine the acceptable practice to honor God and if we should because the concept of God is a concept made-up?

God is a universal word, and it usually comes with worship, honor, and respect for a more superior being other than humanity. We understand that all our concepts belong to a particular category, and we act accordingly. We know that mothers and fathers deserve respect, love, and honor because of the things they have done for their children or cared for because they are seniors, and society has taught us it is our duty.

So, is it so hard to accept the concept of God? Even if the idea is in all the minds of humanity. I cannot say God is not when He is because the concept already exists in my mind. The problem I face is accepting it as an actual value. The value that it is more significant than I am that desires respect, honor, and loyalty more than my vanity.

In closing, nothing can change the reality base of humanity that has already been predesignated. As people with the concept of God in our vocabulary, we know how we must act. Yes, it is hard to believe our physical and mental makeup are set in a course that is impossible to alter from its path. It goes this way as the right way we understand, or it goes this avenue as wrong, which we also cannot deny.

REFERENCE

TAKE A LOOK INSIDE THIS BOOK

1. Ryriel, Charles C. *Dispensationalism*, Chicago, Illinois: Moody Press, 1995 (pgs. 23-41; 195-197).
2. Esposito, John L., Fasching, Darrell, J, & Lewis Todd. *World Religions Today*, New York, NY: Oxford University Press, Inc., 2009.
3. Bowker, John. *God: a brief history*, New York, NY: Dorling Kindersley, Inc., 2003.
4. Hopfe, Lewis M & Woodward, Mark R. *Religions of the World*, Upper Saddle River, New Jersey: Pearson Education Inc., 2009.
5. Johnston, Jerry. Apostasy Now, Jerry Johnston Publishing: Overpark, Kansas, 2007.
6. Richard, Spann J. The Christian Faith and Secularism, New York, NY: Abingdon-Cokesbury Press

A Look Inside This Book Ends.

INTRODUCTION – MAN IN THE WORLD

 Over time, people have wondered how they got here to live on earth, why they are there, and where they will go after their life ends. They have turned to spiritual and non-spiritual teachers for clarity. Biblical teachers have addressed their concerns by enlightening their minds with biblical lessons taken from the Holy Bible. Another way, people have pursued mediums or psychics that do not teach scriptures. Both views can offer individuals guidance about their origin, their reason for existence, and their destiny.

The Holy Bible

Christians, Jews, and Muslims agreed that God inspired writers to author the stories in the Bible. The collections of stories clarify God's interaction with humankind. The many biblical illustrations in the Bible are events that happen over time with God, the Hebrews, and other cultures. The stores' clarifications give accounts of the plan and the purpose of God's authenticity for humanity.

   The Bible books' contents start with five scrolls: the first five books of the Old Testament. They are the Law. Religious authorities have debated and concluded that the Holy Spirit of God moved men over time to author the entire book of the Bible. The division of the Bible consists of two testaments: the Old Testament and the New Testament. They reveal the plan of God for humanity. About "thirty-six authors have written the sixty-six books for about sixteen hundred years." [1]

   The Old Testament tells of the Hebrew race of people's contact with God and their powerless nature to obey His Law. Even so, the "Law" of God had been set, but the sinful nature of people still superseded God's agreements He made with them. People's sinful nature ruled their lives unit the Old Testament's prophecy was fulfilled in the New Testament. In the New Testament, God made a new covenant, which replaced the Old Testament covenant because of the Messiah's birth and death; whom the Christians call Jesus, the Son of God, but the Jew religionists say the Messiah is still to come. Cited from the first five books of the Bible (Psalm 18:22) . [A2]

The Bible is the gateway to God. It gives an excellent outline of how to worship God and how not to offend Him. The central theme of the Bible is to show people how they can live life to stay in the constant flavor of God under God's Plan of Salvation: The concepts of good and evil forces that rule humankind's thoughts. Humankind's responsibility is to understand and know the effects of their minds' two ruling powers. God is a merciful and gracious God who, throughout time, has provided Salvation for humankind, and even if they rejected it, God continues to fulfill His good purposes for humans until evil is excommunicated. The Word of God rules on earth exclusively.

CHAPTER I
DISPENSATIONALISM

The Bible displays biblical points in history called the "eras of dispensations." [2] The start of the eras of dispensations happens initially,
and it will end when time ends. Eras of dispensations point to historical biblical time zones, which indicate God's specific plan of purposes for a particular person or one specific group of people during
a specific period. However, each era of Dispensation set the stage
for humankind's perfection; in most cases, they do not follow God's
agreements or the selected course of the action plan of Salvation.
Even so, God continues to make different platforms to continue to
perfect humanity to live in His domain – The Kingdom of God. The
Kingdom of God is under God's perfect Law, but the Kingdom of
Heaven is the platform to receive the gift of Salvation through the
Holy Spirit, who helps the thoughts of humanity, to be excellent like
their perfect heavenly Father.

The eras of dispensations are called "Dispensationalism." [2]
Dispensationalism is a method of interpreting biblical history that
shows biblical periods' of divisions. God has divided His works and
purposes for humankind into different periods of intervals. Although
some theologians believe in nine eras of dispensations in the Bibles,
other theologians say the count is seven, which this book follows.
The first era of Dispensation is the "Dispensation of Innocence." [2]
At the beginning of time, the Words of God predominated all in the
"Garden of Eden." Cited from Genesis 2:8 [A2].

Dispensation of Innocence

In the Dispensation of Innocent, Adam and Eve were the first
humans on earth, and they lived in this era with no reality of sin
until Satan encouraged them to go against the command of God.
God told them not to eat from the tree of the knowledge of good and

evil. If they did, their spiritual makeup would change, causing them to move into a different reality. According to God's words of absolute rule, their existence was innocent, but when they went against God's commands, a new reality appeared in their minds, causing them to think opposite Words of God.

The Power of the Serpent: In the Garden of Eden, God ruled sole, but serpent had access to the Garden of Eden and Adam and Eve's minds too, but he did not lead either, but he could influence them. He (Satan) told Eve when she eats the fruit of the "tree of knowledge of good and evil," she would become wise like God, and the snake said, that is why God does not want you to eat the fruit. Eve ate the fruit and gave the fruit to Adam, her husband, and he ate it too. They did not understand that when they disobeyed God's command and ate the fruit, they allowed Satan's words to become another reality of ruling authority over their minds. Cited from Genesis 3 [A2]

Now instead of following the Words of God as their reality of good, the existence of evil in their minds was set to follow the commands of Satan's words too. Both concepts are always in conflict with each other. Satan's words are just as powerful in humankind's minds as the Words of God because Satan's opposite words are still a part of God's creative order of words. Remember, God is the creator of all things.

Though God may not condone certain things created under His rule, His words still have total authority over all things. He is the creator of everything. God and Satan do not mix because God does not speak the opposite of His words, even though they are a part of his creation. The Bible affirms that God is not the creator of sin but connects sin in people's lives to bring about "all things to work together for good." Cited from Romans 8:28 [A2].

Dispensation of Conscience

The Dispensation of Innocent changed into the "Dispensation of Conscience" [2] because Adam and Eve choose to disobey God and accept Satan's words. Their tasks to maintain the Garden of Eden and not eat from the tree of knowledge of good and evil, but they did, causing them to leave paradise. The tree of life was there too, and if they were to take and eat its fruit from it, they would live forever in the state of consciousness of sin. God is the Supreme Father of Love, could not continue to allow evil to keep Him from them, but He made a sacrifice that provided them covering for their sin.

In the Dispensation of Conscience, the conscience of human-kind's mind was to respond to God's authority through the meditation of their consciousness. People's responsibility was to maintain self-determination and moral responsibility. The act of obeying God came through their choice of obedience to God's arraignments. During this era of Dispensation, there were three names cited as heroes of faith. They were "Abel, Enoch, and Noah," but others that were mentioned did not respond to the call of God or follow the agreements of God. They were the ones who, of their evil deeds, brought God's judgment on the face of the earth. Cited from Gen. 5 [A2]

Adam and Eve had two sons. Cain, the first son, became a farmer, and Abel, became a herder who looked after the sheep. Adam and Eve still worshipped God and taught their sons to offer sacrifices to Him. Both sons offer a sacrifice unto God, and God accepted one and not the other. Cain became jealous of Abel and killed him because God accepted his brother's sacrifice. God saw Cain had killed Abel, and his sin was judged by God's Law, and a curse falls on him; that he would be a wander and outcast; and the land would not yield its fruit when he tilled the ground. He left the land where Adam and Eve lived and settled in the land of Nod.

The longsuffering of God's love for his creation ended because of wickedness of many people, but one individual found grace in the eyesight of God. Noah responded to God's command and built an ark, in which he, his family, and selected animals of the world entered and remained during the flood. After the flood, God repented and said He would "never destroy the earth again with a flood" and set a rainbow in the sky to remind him of the oath He had pledged to the earth and its inhabitants. Cited, Genesis 9:12-13 [A2]

SIN: The works of Satan are sin, the opposite of the commands of God. On most occasions, God will not perform His works with sin present in a person's life. Sin does not obey God, and it works contrary to the words of God. Humanity's thoughts are of self-will. The influences of their belief are under God's commands to obey His words, or their ideas controlled to obey Satan and disobey God. When they follow their self-will thoughts, they refuse to believe God's words but believe in themselves under the influence of Satan's words. Humanity thinks they can govern themselves and maintain their way of life . They are genuinely wrong because all words are powers of God or Satan, which produce excellent or evil feelings and actions.

Whenever a person desires to follow their sinful nature, that feeling generates an uncontrollable power to fulfill a desire not listed as righteousness. The decisive push of desires can only be controlled with God's divine words. The powered self-willed thoughts of people's minds to accept God's way of thinking is their responsibility. God set the eternal stage for humankind to accept Him as their creator, superior, and protector, but only if they choose. People are not robots.

The Bible uses various terminologies to display the character of humanity's sinful nature. For example, "irreligion; rebellion; treachery; perversion; and abomination are a few," [3] all have different effects and consequences on people and offer judgments from the Law of God. Still, an act of abomination looked at under a powerful microscope. This atrocity is an eyesore, and the punishment is severe because the action is against the natural order of a man and woman.

Sin was studied as the "paradigm method." [3] This method examines human beings' actions or their deeds in a biblical historical setting to determine if the same steps will occur in a non-natural setting. The results draw excellent or evil behavior of the nature of that sin. The act can only go two ways, good or evil because all human actions have set orders of excellent or evil principles that cannot be changed.

Meaning of Sin: The biblical terminology of sin described is "missing the mark." [3] It is an evil action or motive that is in opposition to the Word of God." Sin cannot be replaced with anything else. A sin is an act of "anarchy," an unholy act manifested in the lives of people that is considered an act of aggression against God. Cited by me John 3:4 [A2].

However, non-religious scholars such as "a prominent social-learning theorist, vowed that it is aggressive behavior," [4] that comes about because a person had been exposed to aggression, such as an aggressive in an activity, another person, or an environment. The person exposed to that event caused him to learn that behavior and accepted the experience as part of their norms.

The Judgment of Sin: Humanity's decision to sin will answer to the Law of God. For example, the First Commandment of the Ten Commandments exhorts to humanity that they "shall have no other gods before God." (Exodus 20:2-17). [A2] Another example, Jesus Christ announced that people's thoughts should be centered around "Love the Lord your God with all your heart and with all your soul and with your entire mind and with all your strength." Cited, Deuteronomy, 6:5 [A2]

The Laws of God were revealed to humanity for them to recognize their sinful behavior. Sin is a way of living that shows disrespect to that person and others, and it disregards God's authority. Sin is the major label for all the acts that do not glorify God. For example, hate is a sin. When a person hates it, it opens the door for all other types of sin. Scriptures say, do not let the sun go down on a person when they are angry with another person.

The Cure of Sins: The Bible is the living Word of God. Its words create moral living in the lives of humankind. Throughout the Bible, scriptures reveal the valid Words of God. There are many places in the Bible where God has spoken directly to humanity. In the Old Testament, He spoke directly to prophets, and in the New Testament, Jesus the Son of God. Jesus said He is the Word of God that came down from heaven. In the Bible, people can find spiritual guidance in a time of indecision thinking.

Humanity stands in the middle of a decisive war for their souls. God is believed to have created humans to practice God's love, but some people think they are here to practice a different type of love. The love in the Bible speaks about "agape love in the highest form of love, charity" [5] and "the Love of God for man and man for God."

[5] It is not to be confused with philia love, which is brotherly love, or self-love. Humankind practices religions, psychology, sociology, or philosophies for the cures of their desire to understand the meaning of love. Cited from I Corinthians 12 [A2].

The controlling power of sin is to seek out a need for a desire to fulfill. Sin is a part of humanity's thoughts and feelings that are processed through the mind and body. Sin functions just like everything else that goes through the human mind that activates when a choice of desire has been chosen. Humanity feels sin because sin is a powerful desire or want that pushes flesh to fulfill that desire or want. In most cases, the urges to satisfy that sin are more significant than the desire to choose a God-fearing choice.

The problem with sin is out of control. The sinful nature of humanity is full of all instincts of wrongs. Humanity must want to learn to control them properly. There are three theories about the reasons for sin and the cures of sin. First, "Niebuhr felt sin grows out of the anxiety of finiteness." [6] The need to overcome belongs to one's efforts of the "tension between finiteness and freedom to aspire" [6] to the desire. The cure involves accepting limitations and placing one's confidence in God, but people lack the conversion process and God's knowledge to alter their attitudes.

Another theory for the cures of sins is "Tillich pointed the cure for sin to human existential estrangement." [6] Sin is a natural accompaniment of people's desires, and just like all other influences, there is a matter of choice. In this case, humankind must choose to believe or not believe in the power of sin. Humanity must become increasingly aware of the manner in ways sin projects itself. Sin yeans to their being, the soul of humanity, and it is up to them to discharge that type of behavior.

On the other hand, "Elliott's view cures for sin taken from the "*Premises of Liberation Theology*." [6] He said the cure to eliminate humanity's sinful nature could happen. They are free from oppressions, inequities, and powers that need resolving in the lives of humanity. He also felt the pronouncement of evangelism could take on the economic and political propaganda aimed at altering society's structure." [6] He also looked at "education as a means of eliminating the sinful nature of humankind. He said sin is the antidote that stresses noncompetitive endeavors toward the common goals of all humankind." [6]

Evangelists declared the cures for "humanity's sinful nature is the Word of God. Their nature of the powerful forces seeks to induce them to sin." [6] The supernatural power of God is the cure of sin. The powerful Word of God can alternate humanity's sinful nature. With His hand full of mercies, He helps humankind combat the power of temptations. Humanity's conversion from the carnal mind to the spiritual sense of Christ is the only tangible way for them to fight their sinful desires. The acceptance of Jesus as Savior and Lord can alter people's lives to live under the Plan of God's Salvation. The Holy Spirit's empowerment in their lives makes it possible for people to be empowered to live by God's Word, enter a relationship with Jesus Christ, and put sin away.

SALVATION: Salvation is a way for God to take care of his creation. The Bible gives two facets for the necessity of Salvation: the fact of humankind's evil nature and God's righteousness. God has attempted on many occasions to offer Salvation to humans throughout the Bible. In the Old Testament, the offer came by covenants and the Laws; but in the New Testament, it came with grace and truth believing in the works of Jesus Christ on the cross and His ability to send the Spirit of God back to dwell and act in believers.

Humanity has no power to live righteously to defeat sin in their lives until sealed with the Holy Spirit. The Holy Spirit teaches and guides people to live godly lives. They have the words of eternal life within them, and they are sealed until the day of redemption. Now they have the power to live under the agreements of the covenant of the Law of God. They are empowered to defeat the sinful nature Satan imposed on them.

Throughout history, God has interacted with humanity. The interactions of God with humanity came in many ways to offer them Salvation. At first, God provided Salvation to the first couple Adam and Eve; but it came with obedience. During the Dispensational of Innocent, God told Adam and Eve, "do not eat the fruit from the tree of knowledge of good and evil," but they did, and they experience the effects of the Law of God for disobeying His command. Cited from Genesis 3:9 [A2]

Therefore, because of their newfound knowledge, they experienced a sinful nature in opposition to God's moral character He designed for all humans. The ability and effects of sin continue to be a part of humanity's thoughts and acts even today because Adam and Eve disobeyed God's command. The desires of the sinful nature of society always go against the things of God.

The Salvation of God offered to the next generation was to "Noah." During this time in history, evil influenced humanity's behavior that opposed the ways of good. Their evil ways betrayed the acts of morality, but Noah was a righteous man and believed in God. God commanded him to build an ark big enough to hold him, his family, and selected groups of animals. The entire world except those in ark would cease to exist because of the sins of humanity. The flood covered the face of the earth for 21 days. Cited from Genesis 6:13-22 [A2]

In the ark, Noah, with others, survived the "flood." The command of God against sin let nature release the floodgates of heaven. After the flood and the destruction of a part of humanity. The sons of God sinned because they took daughters of Holy men for wives. In doing so, they bare giants. God said, "Because the Sons of God living on earth were flesh and their days were number hundred and twenty and His Spirit would not always dwell with them." Cited from Genesis 7:1-5 [A2] and Genesis 6:1-3 [A2].

In the land of Nod, Cain had children; one of his children's names was Enoch, a holy and righteous man that did not die like other people, but God took him directly to heaven. Although Enoch was a religious, moral man, his offspring were not, and they displeased God. Men of great physical strength (giants) lived in the land and did not recognize God in a holy and righteous way. They married the daughters of Enoch. God was displeased and said," humans are not angels, and my spirit will not remain with them forever since they are flesh." Cited from Genesis 6:1-8 [A2].

Next, God sought out "Abraham" in a distant land and offered him Salvation too, and in return, Abraham needed to have a form of faith to believe in God. Abraham believed in God and became the father of the faith of Israel. He became the father of faith for many countries, the church, and the entire world. Today "He is the basis of faith to believe the message of Jesus Christ sent from God to the entire world." For "without faith, it is impossible to please God." Cited from Genesis 12:1-3 and Hebrew 6 [A2].

Abraham's faith opens the heart of both Jews and Gentiles to believe that Jesus Christ is the Son of God who came into the world to offer humanity the Salvation of God. The fulfillment of the Old Testament's prophecy proclaimed, "God would live among men" (Emmanuel) to fulfill the Old Testament's covenants and prophecies through Jesus Christ. Cited from Matthew 1:23 [A2] God offered Salvation first to Israel, but they did not receive it because of disbelief. The prophecy fulfilled in the New Testament spoke of the Salvation of Israel's God now offered to the gentiles. Humanity received this gift of God because the Jews rejected it. Now all of humanity can have Salvation for believing in Jesus Christ as the world's Savior. Notes: From Matthew 1:23 [A2].

The Nation of Israel professed and still professes that their interaction of religious faith is of the One True God. Their story told in the Old Testament (Tora) tells of the sacred scribes' inscription of the covenants and God's promises; God made with them. The nation of Israel righteously speaks of its history of salvation. Their story tells of their encounters with God throughout their lives. Now God offers covenants and commitments to the world. The covenants and promises are all in the name of Jesus. To believe that Jesus Christ is the Son of God, and He came to this world to teach humanity God's ways and die as a sacrificial sacrifice to defeat the indifferent powers of God that reign over humanity's thoughts. Jesus came in a body of man's sinful nature to assure that humanity can live righteous God-fearing lives, and power over the nature of sin.

COVENANTS: The meaning of the Old Testament covenants is to establish "an enduring commitment to God based on mutual vows of loyalty and mutual obligations. The ratification agrees that both parties have fellowship." [7] The symbolic meaning of covenants of God is binding keys placed in an individual(s) heart(s) always to reserve a place of assurance, confidence, and love that God will fulfill His covenant promises. A person(s) in covenant with God understand God's covenant of good that last forever.

The eyes of God looked upon humanity in two dimensions, in flavor, when they follow in the path of His directions or commands, and disfavor when they do not obey His instructions. When people are in God's favor, they are under His covenant protection. Throughout the Bible, God has established covenants with certain people(s) and nation(s). In most cases, the establishment of a covenant happens during an era of dispensation. Within each covenant, God establishes specific ways for people(s) to obey His commands, worship Him, and live a lifestyle pleasing Him. Covenants are made explicitly for that person or group of people in a specific way, which are made according to that time in history.

Covenant liaison with God: God's covenants offered protection, and He expects in return compliance with the conditions of the treaty. There are various categories of covenants. There are four "Covenants of Community." [6] The four covenants of the community each play a part during a specific period. The task is to bring a person(s) into a genuine covenant of salvation relationship with God.

The first covenant of community was with Noah. After the flood that destroyed all of humanity except Noah, his family, and individual animals. God promised (covenant) to never destroy the earth with a flood. God made a covenant with Abraham too. God promised Abraham a son in his old age, and he believed in God. Abraham is known as the father of faith for the universe. The covenant outlines, "Without faith, it is impossible to please or come near to God." God sealed the covenant with the circumcision of all the males in Abraham's household. He told him that he and his descendants must always worship Him as the one true God. Cited from Hebrew 11:6-8 [A2]

God signed the Sinai covenant at Mount Sinai, right after Israel was delivered from the bondage of Egypt. He said, "Now, therefore, if you obey my voice and keep my covenant, you shall be a treasured possession out of all the people" … a priestly kingdom and a holy nation." The Old Testament's last covenant is with King David, and

God promised David offspring would always reign as kings in Israel. But in the New Testament, under the rule of the New Covenant, Jesus is the King of Kings that reigns as the King of Israel (Church too) instead of one of David's offspring. Cited from Exodus 19:5-6 [A2].

Finally, three covenants represent the "Covenants of Salvation." [7] The first of the three covenants governing the relationship between God and Israel, is the Sinai Covenant of Promise. The next is the Covenant of the Law. This covenant defined sin and brought light to the sinful behaviors of people as unacceptable practices. The Covenant of Promise, the Promise of the Holy Spirit. This covenant promised a guide and comforter that would come to change the hearts of the people toward God. Even though all three of the covenant agreements are different, they all represent covenant obligations; if broken, the covenant agreements become nude and void.

THE LAW OF GOD The Pentateuch is a Greek word that means five scrolls. The Old Testament's scrolls are the first five books of the Bible called the Law of Moses. It consists of the origin of life and the introduction of God's involvement in humanity's lives. It tells of the Hebrew people's experiences of covenant relationships with God and their responsibility to educate other races about the knowledge they obtain about God.

The Law is a set way of doing things, and if broken, there are penalties to be paid. The Hebrew people in the Old Testament played significant roles that keep records of their interactions with God. One of their records recorded that Moses received the Laws of God directly from the hand of God. Their record-keeping carries on the story of life with God.

The first covenant God made was with Adam and Eve. He told Adam, "From every tree in the garden you are free to eat, but from the tree of the knowledge of good and evil you must not eat; for the day that you eat of it you shall certainly know death." They disobeyed God and ate, and in doing so, they disputed the covenant agreements with God. Through many eras of dispensations, humankind finally came to live on the platform to receive the promise God made to Adam and Eve in the Garden of Eden. The Lord said to the snake, one of your offspring (Satan) will strike her offspring (Jesus) on the heel, and one of her offspring (Jesus) will hit him (Satan) on the head. Jesus fulfilled the promise in the New Testament. "Jesus' line of His genealogy" is traced to Mary, not Joseph because Jesus' Father is God. Cited from Genesis 2:17 [A2], Genesis 3:14-15 [A2],

More than six hundred law codes in the Laws written in Exodus, Leviticus, Numbers, and Deuteronomy reveal God's Laws. The books are to "maintain order and regulate civil" obedience. Besides, "religions, and "ceremonial, and criminal justice life of Israel per the holiness necessary for maintaining the covenant relation of God's, with Israel." [2] The Old Testament Law defined the covenant situations for life living the Hebrew community. Cited from the Old Testament [A2]

The outline of the first five books of the Old Testament is shown below:

Genesis: "The agreement of a covenant promises, election of Abraham, and providential preservation of his family."

Exodus: "Miraculous deliverance of God's people from bondage in Egypt, covenant the relationship expanded to Israel as the people at Sinai, and the Law of God was given to Israel."

Leviticus: "Covenant expansion of the Law for holiness among the people of God, since He will dwell in their midst."

Numbers: "Testing, purging, a purifying of God's covenant people in the Sinai wilderness."

Deuteronomy: "Covenant renewal and the Law giving as preparation for entry into the land of the promise of the second generation of God's people."

Note: Taken from the first five books of the Holy Bible

Covenants, Laws, Precepts, or Ordinance: God's agreements cover specific living agreements in the Old Testament. It is hard to determine if the deals centered around living arrangements of man's versions of God. Still, Jesus rebukes the Pharisees on many occasions about rituals they deemed essential and acts against God. However, the Ten Commandments are certainly Laws of God.

Jesus said He did not come to change the Law but to fulfill it. The content of Matthew Chapter Five centered on the teachings of Jesus. The profound statement up heals excellent controversy. What did He mean by the word, " I did not come to change the Law? The five different instructions in the chapter give ways to understand what he meant by the statement.

The Law of God set the stage for an agreement of a covenant. The Law sets the stage to see the differences between sin and righteousness. The teachings of Jesus formed a different attitude toward the Law and disregarded the Law-breaking but learned to correct it in loving situations.

The Sermon on the Mouth (3-12) are the Similitudes that advises keeping oneself full of grace and beauty to glorify God on a tedious and challenging bearing journey (13-16). Relation of Christ to the Law (17-20). *Jesus taught that the Law stands as it is, and if broken, the same judgment imposed* first reconciliation, then sacrifice (21-26). Be at peace with one another always. Always take care of this first before offering a gift on the altar. Lust, adultery, and Divorce (chapters. 27-32.), and Perjury and Retaliation are forbidden (33-42). Tolerate enemies with love and peace. (43-48). Be perfect as God is perfect in heaven, for He gives food to everyone, good or evil, so be like Him, do good to everyone.

CHAPTER II
DISPENSATIONALISM
CONTINUES

Dispensation of Conscience

Dispensation of Conscience is the second era of the dispensation that happened right after Adam and Eve could no longer continue to be residents in the Garden of Eden. This era of dispensation continued until after the flood wiped out all humanity except Noah, his family, and individual animals. During this time in history, humankind was the ruler of their conscience. They became incest with self-gratification and immorality. One out of many aspects of this dispensation is the Promise of Christ the Savior. God promised this to the woman right after they had sinned, and His Law gave judgment on their iniquity. He said a savior will be born from a woman's seed and will have the power to "bruise the serpent's head" (Satan), and He (Jesus Christ) would resign in his place. Cited from Genesis 3:15 [A2].

Dispensation of Human Government

The third era of the Dispensation of Human Government. This indulgence started after the Great Flood of Noah's time that destroyed all humanity except Noah, his family, and individual animals. They were saved from the flood because they entered the ark designed by God. They and the creatures were to populate the world again. God made to Noah and the earth's habitations a promise that He would "never destroy the earth with a flood." Cited from Genesis 4:12 [A2].

After Noah and his descendants settled on earth, God told them to scatter across the land and replenish it, but they did not obey His command. About "325 years" [2] after the flood, the earth's inhabitants began to take pride in selves and said they wanted to reach heaven. They tried to build a tower to reach heaven, but God ruined their plans when He caused them to speak to one another in different languages. Thus, God stopped the builders from the building of the tower, and they left and scattered across the face of the earth to fulfill God's command to fill the world." The result of them scattered across the planet was the rise of different nations and cultures. "From that point on, human governments took the place of the rule of the Kingdom of God. The rule of human governments is the ruling reality of people ever since." Cited from Genesis 11:7-9 [A2].

Dispensation of Promise

The fourth dispensation is called the Dispensation of Promise. The dispensation lasted about "430 years." [2] God call Abraham out of his country of Ur of the Chaldeans' land to travel a distance to worship Him in the land of Canaan. This dispensation continued through the lives of the patriarchs. It ended with the departure of the Jewish people from Egypt. During this time, God created a great nation that He had chosen as His people. God established the "Abrahamic Covenant." The covenant would fulfill God's promise that "Abraham would be the father of faith" for many cultures. Cited from Genesis 12:1–Exodus 19:25 [A2].

Dispensation of the Mosaic Law

The fifth dispensational era is called the Dispensation of Law of the Old Testament. "This dispensation lasted about 1,500 years." [2] The duration of this dispensation lasted from the nation of Israel's exodus from Egypt until it voids after Jesus Christ's death. During the Dispensation of Law, God established a covenant with the Jewish nation called the Mosaic Covenant. During this dispensation, "the contact spoke persons of God were prophets." [2]

The object of Israel 's journey through the wilderness was to get them ready to enter the "promised land." Still, due to the people's disobedience of the covenant agreements, they did not reach their homeland, the promise of God. The generation that left Egypt never made it to the new land but died in the wilderness, and a new generation replaced them and received the covenant promises of God. They entered the new land rich with natural resources under the protection of God. Cited from Exodus 19:1-Joshua 24:33 [A2].

Dispensation of Grace

The sixth era of dispensation happens in the Dispensation of Grace. A new covenant went into effect made with the blood of Christ. (Luke 22:20) The "Age of Grace" or "Church Age occurs between the 69th and 70th week of Daniel 9:24." [2] It illustrates the coming of the Spirit on the Day of Pentecost, the start of the church, and ends with the rapture of the church (1 Thess. 4). The dispensation is worldwide and includes both Jews and the Gentiles. The Dispensation of Grace is active right now. God will forgive the unlawful acts of humankind if they confess their sins are against Him, and believe His Son is His Word.

Humanity's responsibility during the Dispensation of Grace is to believe in the teaching of Jesus, and He is the Son of God (John 3:18). In this dispensation, "the Holy Spirit indwells in believers as the comforter," counselor, and guide (John 14:16-26). "This dispensation has lasted for almost 2,000 years. No one knows when it will end." [2] It is believed it will end when believers are raptured from the earth to heaven with Christ. Following the rapture, the judgment of God occurs, which will last for seven years. During the Dispensation of Grace, the Church is the ruling authority of God.

The Dispensation of the Millennium

The seventh dispensation era is called "the Millennial Kingdom of Christ." [2] This dispensation will last for 1,000 years as Christ Himself rules on earth. This Kingdom will fulfill the prophecy to the Jewish nation that Christ will return and be their King. "The only people allowed to enter the Kingdom are the born-again believers from the Age of Grace, righteous survivors of the seven years of tribulation, and the resurrected Old Testament saints." [2] During this time of peace, the church's adversary Satan bounded during the 1,000 years. This period ends with the final judgment. Cited from Revelation 20:11-14 [A2]

CHAPTER III
ORIGINALITIES OF
HUMANITY

Many positions explain how humankind came into existence. The two most considered are creation and evolution. Creationists say the story of design gives the right answer. It provides an accurate record of the beginning of life on earth. Creationists use the Holy Bible's first chapter to illustrate that God created the heavens and the world, and then He created people. Cited from Genesis Chapters 1-2 [A2].

On the other hand, is the theory of evolution? Evolutionist affirms that humankind's beginning evolved from a single "cell." [9] The cell evolved into all living and non-living substances such as humankind and all other things on earth. They say the evolution of humanity happened naturally when the material world interacted. They believe in a community where the residents fight for resources and the strongest survive and evolve.

CREATION: The scriptures start with "the creation of God." God created the heavens, the earth, and all living things such as people. The thoughts of humankind set the stage for their reality of all existence on earth, and they hold the only method to contact God. Humankind believes God converses with them to fulfill their needs and command their responsibilities. Christians teach that the Bible is the only source that genuinely gives the Words of God. They say the Bible guilds them to live a life that pleases Him, and that provides the information of God for people to live a safe life from the oppositional powers of Satan. Cited from Genesis: 1-3 [A2]

The scriptures give examples for people to follow to fulfill God's covenant agreements, and for protection from their adversary and God's adversary, the enemy, a former archangel in the Assembly of God. He is set to war against God, using the opposite Words of God. Christians call him the devil or Satan, or Lucifer. Therefore, to sum up, the story of creation boils down to the battle, between the righteous of God or Satan's evilness and the winners and the losers.

Accordingly, to the scriptures, the winners go to heaven, a place prepared by God full of joy and peace, or the losers go to hell with Satan, a place that burns with fire and the taste for want of life that never ceases. People can choose to believe that Jesus is the Son of God that sent the Holy Spirit to seal them to go into a righteous afterlife. According to the Promise of God, the lifestyles of living to honor God showed in love, will be judged to determine if they can enter the gates of heaven.

EVOLUTION: Evolution is an impression of biology. "Biological evolution deals with a particular type of change through time." [8] Charles Darwin and many others discovered that plants and animals live in communities. He also noticed that individual animals' lifeline survives after the duration of living serials of lives. Darwin said that species in a community evolve into something different from their original makeup. For example, he believed that the "human race evolved from apes." [8]

Darwin's Theory of Evolution: Charles Darwin (1809–1882), an English naturalist, founded the evolution theory. Evolution is a biological evolution theory that discusses the development of man and all existence of life. This theory states all "species are organisms developed through the natural selection of small, inherited variations (cell) that increase individuals' ability to compete, survive, and reproduce." [9]

The theory of evolution states, "the origin of humankind is in line with the evolution of his environment." [9] Evolution is a theory of science. Darwin argued that the variety of organisms comes about by the evolution of the species. He continued to explain the formation of man's lifeline of progress, which provided a particular means that account for human development. The theory of evolution came from researching the biology of the human body and environmental species. The material revealed the human makeup comes from traces of evolutionary origin. His theory accounted for ancestral development and the continuum developmental cycle of humankind." [9] The evidence of Darwin's evolution theory found from extinct fossils of organisms showed some species were not suitable to make a change.

Darwin wrote three topics (books) about the evolution of man. He first wrote about the "origin of the species." [10] In Darwin's book, "the *Origin of Species*" (1859), Darwin read Malthus's essay on the "*Principle of Population*." He realized that if more species lived and reproduced in an environment, the overall survival rate would have to compete for food, living space, and other limited necessities of life. He determined that the best competing species would be the one to survive.

He continued to explain his belief that humans evolved. In his thesis, the *survival of the fittest*, he wrote, "mankind is not a product of creation." [10] In the theory of survival of the fittest, he proposed a struggle for existence among all species. He saw in an environment that species connected between species with variations and adaptation interests in the background. He agreed that species' heritable characteristics increased their chances for survival and reproduction in their environment. He concluded his research with the idea that every living organism has a desire to complete to survive

Darwin's theory on the survival of the fittest explained that species that adapt well to their environment have a high chance of reproducing more and are more likely their offspring will survive. On the other hand, species with characteristics that are not well suited to their environment could be due to their inability to reproduce. They produce few offspring, and it is a probability the offspring will not survive in the community.

Natural Selection: The "theory of Natural Selection" [11] is a process that species can survive and reproduce in an environment. However, if the environmental conditions change unfavorably, those species may no longer be suitable to stay. For example, "the conditions of environmental change may be faster than the species can adapt to those changes, which can cause the species to become extinct." [11] Natural selection sees the conditions of an environment and determines if that species can adapt to the environment is the only means of its survival.

Evolution is the story of the man and his environment, the theory of science. The advance draws its conclusion about humanity from facts gathered, observed, and determined that those facts are sound truths. Science is the study of the natural world and universe founded on what scientists learned from observation and experiments." [10]

Evolution affirmed humankind evolved from a single cell: For example, the cell reproduces and becomes a man. The theory of evolution states that all living substances and matters of the earth consist of DNA. DNA writes the instructions for what all things will become. One question that scientists try to answer is what caused the fashion of humankind. For example, the first thing scientists consider is what they have learned from their practices in the world. Their personal experience consists of their consciousness of their past and factors that affect their present. They also observed species' interactions in an environment, such as people, animals, or insects.

The Scientific Method: Proposing a Hypothesis: https://courses.lumenlearning.com/boundless-biology/chapter/the-science-of-biology/01/14/2021

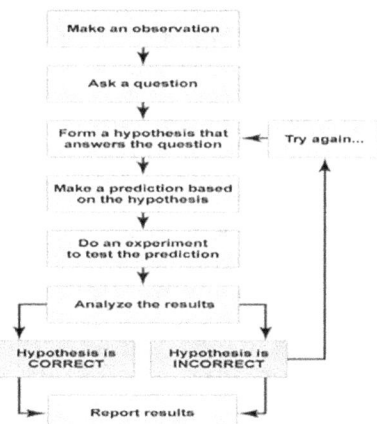

CHAPTER IV
WHY ARE PEOPLE
LIVING ON EARTH?

There are two reasons people live on earth: to get to know God, and the other is to get to know others. The Bible gives the picture that people created to glorify God. They are to worship God, treat others properly, and live a moral lifestyle. Even so, secularism, a nonreligious practice, believes that people are here to do good without harm and no God intervention.

In the book of Genesis, God said, "Lets us make man in our image, after our likeness: and let them have dominion over the fish of the sea and the fowl of the air, and over the cattle, and all the earth, and over every creeping thing that crepe upon the earth." God gave man absolute rule over overall existence on the earth, allowing him to name them and say what they are, based on the type of behavior they performed. In the thoughts of God, He created humanity in His image and gave them dominion over the entire earth, suggesting that they should act in the capacity of Him, but under His, Law to govern the world. Cited from Genesis 3 [A2].

To maintain the earth and populate, God, blessed both Adam and Eve and said to them. "Be fruitful, and multiply, and replenish the earth and subdue it. He gave them dominion over the fish of the sea, and the fowl of the air, and over every living thing that moves upon the earth." Their work details were the upkeep of the trees and plants to provide scenic beauty and maintain the food supply, but God said do not eat from the tree of the knowledge good and evil, or you will know sin and die. Cited from Genesis 3 [A2].

God told Adam and Eve in the Garden of Eden to be "fruitful and become many." He gave them one command. "You must not eat from the tree of the knowledge of good and evil, for when you eat of it, you will die." The moral of the story is the instructions of God for them not to "eat the fruit of the tree of knowledge of good and evil to not experience death. God created people to have the free exercise of their will. They were placed in the Garden of Eden to be fruitful, multiply themselves, and relish the earth. Cited from Genesis 3 [A2].

Death experience twice: A spiritual death happens when a person does not practice morality anymore and refuses to obey and worship God. The second type of death is physical; it occurs when a person dies. Both ends represent human abnormality when a change in life happens, and humanity finds itself living at a different stage of life.

There are tales about the sins of Adam and Eve eating the fruit. One theory states that the fruit seeds gave them a sexual desire. That is a false statement because God told them to procreate, and the only way the people could do that is to have sex. Still, others have said eating the fruit could give them the knowledge to understand evil. The statement does hold some truth. The scripture stated they were innocent until they ate the fruit, and their eyes were open. Disobeying God's command is more severe than eating the fruit, so disobedience caused them to sin, and eating the fruit caused them to be like God, knowing good and evil.

The Book of Genesis tells of the rebel of humanity to live under the authority of God. Under the rule of God, people were responsible for their conduct. They had to live according to the righteous Law of God. They decided to build a tower to reach God. God said if they reach heaven, then they would think they are gods and rule in that capability. He scattered them across the face of the earth. Today over thirty-nine different governments rule the lives of people.

To Develop Governments to Maintain Environments: The twenty different forms of governments vary in the ruing styles over people's lives. For example, in the United States of America, the economy is based on a free market where anyone can bargain. Other countries' environment runs according to their economy, too. In addition, in most economies, the political system governs the economy, military power, and citizens' positions. Jesus announces His Kingdom is not of this world; it has no political forces or ruling parties. People accept the gift of Salvation, and the Holy Spirit will teach and lead them to how to be citizens in the Kingdom of God.

Government Systems in the World

Anarchy "governs its people without support of the government. The division of society is divided into different, locally ruled settlements. Examples are the absence of public utilities, a lack of regulatory control, and limited diplomatic relations with other nation-states." [A1]

Aristocracy "rules its people of lower socioeconomic strata under the power of wealthy nobles. It promotes an inherent class system that connects wealth and ethnicity with both the ability and right to rule. An example is they obtain an education, nurture, and genetic traits required for rulership." [A1]

Bureaucracy is "a form of government that directs its people usually under the rule of a dictator or a democracy. Its people function under non-elected government officials. Their public responsibilities are dictated by administrative policy-making groups that obey rules, regulations, procedures, and outcomes formulated to maintain order, achieve efficiency, and prevent favoritism within the system." [A1]

Capitalism promotes "an economic idea of open competition and the belief that a free market economy (one with limited regulatory control) is the most efficient form of economic organization. Some say that capitalism promotes economic growth, improved living standards, higher productivity, and broader prosperity. In contrast, others argue that capitalism inherently promotes inequality, exploitation of the labor class, and unsustainable use of resources and land." [A1]

Colonialism is "a nation that extends its sovereignty over other territories. In practice, this often entails Indigenous populations' occupation and the exploitation of resources to benefit the ruling nation. The colonizer imposes its economy, culture, religious order, and form of government on its people to strengthen its authority." [A1]

Communism's idea of a gov. refers to "the idea of common, public ownership of the economy, including infrastructure, utilities, and means of production. Communism often incorporates the idea of revolutionary action against the unequal rule. Communism often positions itself as a counterpoint to the economic stratification underlying capitalism. The resistance to stratification sometimes takes the form of a single-state authority, one in which political opposition or dissent may restrict that country's residence. Some communist states are a more despotic form of governance, as typified by the Soviet brand of communism that swept the globe during the mid-20th century." [A1]

Democracy is a form of government that "the people are empowered when elect officials to office. They elect their leaders believing they will receive fair representation, a system in which no single force can exercise unchecked control or authority. The result is a system that requires discourse, debate, and compromise to satisfy the broadest number of public interests." [A1]

Federalism "combines and divides powers between a centralized federal authority and regional and local authorities. This is a system in which a set of states, territories, or provinces are both self-governing and accountable to the authority of a general, unifying government structure. This is considered a balance in the approach that provides the equal status of authority to two distinct levels of government. [A1]

Feudalism is "a social structure that revolves around land ownership, nobility, and military obligation. Feudalism refers to a way of life in which sharp, hierarchical divisions separate noble classes, clergy, and peasantry, opportunities for movement between these hierarchies. In this system, peasants typically provided labor and military service in exchange for occupancy of land and protection from outside forces" [A1]

In a Kleptocracy, "the government's ruling party has either come to power or retained power, through means of corruption and theft. The form of government that a ruling class would ever self-apply but a pejorative term used to describe a group whose power rests on a foundation of embezzlement, misappropriation of funds, and the transfer of massive amounts of wealth from public to private interests. These private interests will typically overlap the ruling party's economic interests." [A1]

Meritocracy is "a system in which authority is vested in those who have demonstrated the merits deemed pertinent to governing. These merits are often conferred through testing and academic credentials meant to create an order in which talents, abilities, and intellect determine who should hold leadership and economic stewardship positions. The result is a social hierarchy based on achievement." [A1]

Military Dictatorship rules under "a single authority figure with absolute power. The military dictatorship heads the nation's armed forces. The power to rule often comes by subverting the existing seat of government — sometimes though claims of corruption, weakness, or ineffectiveness use of the military to establish its law and order." [A1]

Monarchy is ruled due by "a single member of a royal bloodline with absolute power and authority. The individual in the seat of power is placed there by "divine right," or the will of God. In a monarchical society, power is inherited within a succession line related to one's bloodline bordered within the line royal family. However, until the 19th century, the monarchy was the most usual form of government in the world." [A1]

An oligarchy is a form of government in which "a smattering of individuals rules over a nation. Oligarchs are catch-all for any number of other forms of governance. A specific set of qualities — wealth, heredity, race — are used to vest power in a small group of individuals. There are forms of government as aristocratic, plutocratic, or totalitarian that are referred to as oligarchic. Oligarchies are characterized by tyrannical or authoritarian rule and an absence of democratic practices or rights." [A1]

Plutocracy is "a system of rulers in which power determines its direct function of wealth. Plutocracy runs the economy under a hierarchy of the aristocratic system. It lacks the philosophical imperatives used to justify the latter. Aristocratic forms of governance justified economic hierarchy by presuming equivalence between wealth, heredity to say lead qualification. Plutocracy refers to the ascendance of the wealthy to positions of power." [A1]

Republicanism form of government refers to "a system in which power is vested in the citizenry. In technical definition, a republic is a nation where the people hold popular sovereignty through the electoral and legislative processes through participation in public and civic life. In its earliest form, the republic was perceived as a counterbalance to monarchy, an approach, which merged monarchy and aristocracy with some trappings of democracy." [A1]

Socialism is a form of government in which "the people own the primary means of production. Socialism is provident compassing public services such as universal healthcare. By contrast, In the less compromising and often more authoritarian nature of communism, socialism tends to be a malleable concept. Some adherents view socialism as a strict policy of shared ownership and equal distribution of resources, while others believe free-market capitalism can coexist with socialist forms of public administration. To wit, the Social Security system of the declaratively capitalist United States is inherently socialist." [A1]

Theocracy refers to a form of government in which "a specific religious ideology informs the leadership, laws, and customs. In many instances, there will be little to no distinction between scriptural laws and legal codes. Likewise, religious clergy will typically occupy leadership roles, and in some instances, the highest office in the nation. Because religious law usually extends from writings and traditions that are many centuries old and therefore, impose practices that may not conform to present-day standards of ethical justice or constitutional law, theocracies frequently run afoul of organizations and agencies advocating for global human rights." [A1]

Totalitarianism is an authoritarian form of government in which "the ruling party recognizes no limitations whatsoever on its power, either in the public life or private rights of its citizens. Power is vested in the hands of a single figure, an authority around which effective propaganda is built as a way of extending and retaining uncontested authority. Totalitarian states often employ widespread surveillance, control over mass media, intimidating demonstrations of paramilitary or police power, and suppression — usually violent — of protest, activism, or political opposition." [A1]

Tribalism refers to a form of "governance in which central authority is absent, and instead, various regional tribes lay claim to different territories, resources, or domains. In this system, trade, commerce, and war may occur between different tribes without the involvement or oversight of a unifying structure. The prevalent way of life in the premodern world is where different families and clans establish common rules and rituals specific to their community. While many tribes have internal leadership forms — from councils and chiefdoms to warlords and patriarchs — tribes are also distinct for having limited role differentiation or role stratification. In some regards, this can make the customs internal to some tribes, particularly egalitarian. That said, tribalism as a way of life that threatens many parts of the world extinguished, by modernity, development, and the imposition of outside authority." [A1]

The Rule of Economies/Governments

The twenty different forms of governments vary in the ruling styles over the people's lives and the environment. For example, in the United States of America, the economy is based on a free market where anyone can bargain. Other countries' environment runs according to their economy, too. Still, in most countries, the economy is not run as a free economy, where everybody across the world can trade and buy. In most economies the political system governs the economy, with military power.

The dogma of secularism: Most governments, except for a few, rule their government under the ideology of secularism. Secularism believes "religious ideology should not be a part of political or civic affairs or in running public institutions, special schools." [12] The faith of people to put their trust in the invisible things. A scientific explanation is more prevalent in explaining life's difficulties than just following God's Ten Commandments. Thus, most attitudes about religions are considered a "post-religious Christian philosophy." [12]

Humanism rule of government: Another ideology that some governments rule under is humanism. Humanism is another system of thought that leaves out the supernatural authority of God. It replaces it with human values, characteristics, and behaviors believed to bring out the best human beings. People's outlook on life is based on their survival, and theories such as evolution, secularism, and humanism explain life's competitive struggle. People best tailored in life to compete will survive.

Effective Challenge of Christianity to Secularism: What the church needs to compete against the achievements of science and technology, the arts, national power, and the worldwide economic structure of secularism. The Church must show the world it is what they need, but to fill those shoes, the church must perform the duties that God instill in her to do. The Church's mission is to spread the good news by telling others about Jesus Christ's works on the cross and live by His teaching. Salvation is a gift of God. The gift is there for the taking of anybody, but there are works that must be performed.

The Church is the Ruling Power on Earth

The Bible is the sword of the spirit; it cut the rights, the wrongs, and the evil asunder. The Church can only be the leader of the world when it chooses to work on the side of God. The side of God is following scriptures of the Holy Bible and nothing else. Humankind cannot reason to believe God's will to make things better according to their reasoning. Following God's formal agreements, believers do not need precision because God's Law is written for them to follow.

The Church must recognize and not participate in secularism and call it out for idolatry. Idolatry will always turn out to be an impoverishment to offend rather than enrich it. Faith in secularism proposed to help people be better; they claim it follows the same religious principle, except it leaves out to honor the Supreme Being.

The principles of God are seen in the teachings of Jesus Christ. Jesus teaches the reflection of God's things; his expectations of believers are to exhibit righteous living. The ones who want to be participants in the Kingdom of Heaven will follow the guidelines and believe it will work. The Christians base their hope, their faith, and belief in Jesus. Jesus is the way, the truth, and the light. There is no other way to come through the door to get to God except through Jesus. This is what the Church must believe. God did not tell the Church to accept what he deemed unacceptable, but they must reprove it. Sin is sin; the teaching of secularism is a corruption of the Word of God.

Church must accept it for what it is: The Church is supposed to be the world's ruling government, but many churches have taken on secularism. Their way puts constraints on the rites of the Church's operations. It is now time for the Church to call on God's powers, become prayer warriors, and organize into a stronghold of Christian believers for one purpose and one purpose only. That is to glorify God and live according to the Words of Jesus Christ.

The traditions of the Church cannot take sides with secularism or humanistic principles. The Church is not the ruling factor of its existence or power, but God. The Salvation of God is based on God's Law or commands, and if they are followed, the Church can see God's power manifest itself in the Church. The principles of secularism ideology are based on the reasoning of humanity. For example, the five principles of Utilitarianism are vastly different from Christianity's faith statement.

The Three Principles that Serve as the Basic Axioms of Utilitarianism:

1. Pleasure or utilitarianism is the term "utility", which in this context does not mean "useful" [11] but, instead, means pleasure or happiness. John Stuart Mill (1806-1873) argued that people never value anything unless they associate it in some way with pleasure or happiness." [13] Thus, they appreciate beauty because it is pleasurable to behold. They value knowledge because it helps cope with the world's problems and links them to happiness. They value love and friendship because they bring sources of pleasure and satisfaction to their lives.

2. Actions are right as far as they promote happiness; wrong as far as they produce, unhappiness seems quite sensible. "The principle is controversial. For example, a gift offering of $1,000 to a charity, expect a sense of duty in return. Pleasure and happiness, though, are unique in being valued purely for their own sake. There is no other reason to love them except the need to be satisfied." [14] The view is, that it is better to be happy than sad, the reality cannot prove to offer any value.

3. Everyone's happiness counts equally. The apparent moral principle, but when put forward by Jeremy Bentham (1748-1832). He looked at life in the form of, "everyone to count for one; no one for more than one," [14] is radical thinking. For example, Over two hundred years ago, this idea was held as a standard view. The view is that some lives and the happiness they contain are simply more important and valuable than others. The lives of masters were more important than slaves

Religious Teachings: The use of the Holy Bible throughout history has been one means to understand the way to communicate with God, to understand His purposes for humankind, and to show people how to respect and love God as the Supreme Being. The Bible is a tool to teach people what will happen if they do this or if they do not do that. The Bible is the Law of God that outlines what is fitting them to do and what they should not be or do, and if broken, this is what the outcome or penalty of the consequences will render.

Challenge of Non-Religious Teachings: The Bible has been the number one lead for people to understand the spiritual guides to follow God's principles for their roles and purposes while living on earth. However, over the last decades, people's beliefs in God's biblical teachings have decreased to encourage enough concern for considering a historical theological systematic analysis of what is going on in a non-religious setting.

There are many non-religious beliefs: The strategy is to influence people's minds to believe there is no God's ruling authority. Secular thought gives knowledge and power to people that do not include God. They believe they are knowledgeable enough to maintain their lives without God. One type of secular teaching is utilitarianism: Its announcement is a secular thought. Secularism has been around in the education circle since the Reformation Period. The overall concept of utilitarianism is happiness without harm.

Compatibility of Utilitarianism and Christianity: Utilitarianism is considered an ethical doctrine. Its outlook is that "the greatest happiness of the greatest number should be the criterion of the virtue of action." [13] In many respects, it is the outlook of David Hume, writing in the mid-18th century. However, it received both its name and its most explicit statement in Jeremy Bentham's writings (1748-1832) and John Stuart Mill (1806-1873). Mill believes people should think and feel happiness as consisting of many and varied pleasures. Even today, Mill's essay Utilitarianism remains one of the most widely taught expositions of the doctrine.

The teaching of utilitarianism is about how people resolve ethical issues –. Their technique is the separation of options such as two desirable objectives or two evils, or a given situation where there is both a positive and a negative aspect. They use a type of measurement in the processes. For example, the solution determined, that "the value that is sought to be maximized in any given situation is to involve a choice." [14] In other words, the "idea of the greatest happiness of the greatest number" [12] so a person knows whether the idea is achievable.

Utilitarianism Defense of Having the Nature of Christianity: Rev William Paley (1806-1873), a utilitarian, wrote his arguments on utilitarianism's compatibility with Christianity. His approach was to confront specific conventional objections to utilitarianism belief. He used science to compare ethics to Christianity's ethics. His thought of Christianity was an "organized corpus of ideas which was internally consistent." [14] He affirmed that there are "certainly motives that rule the results in the whole edifice, and that fit together within a set of logical rules so that the greatest utility produced if humanity is motivated to follow God's will (the rules) rigidly." [13] The outcome of utilitarianism is the by-product if people will follow God. Therefore, "Christianity is compatible with utilitarianism, and if a functional result is not achieved, people have not obeyed God." [13]

Paley started with God's will and the outcome of a person's intention to explain his "reasoning investigate motive." [14] The question he sought after was, "why am I obliged to do what is right: to act agreeably to the fitness of things: to conform to reason, nature or truth: to promote the public good or to obey the will of God?" [14] For example, He used the obligation of the urged of a violet motive at the expense of another. The expectation of a reward or punishment for a violent reason happens in this life; "therefore, private happiness is our motive and the rule" [14] of the will of God.

Paley used utilitarianism as a bond with God to show it as the object of God's will. He said humanity must follow God's will. The two methods society can be obedient to God's will, first, used scripture to declare the God of Christianity's mind – he purposed this could happen when God expresses orders that come out of scriptures.

Secondly, he used the disposition of God's design of His works or His design of nature, declaring God's results needed clarification and going beyond scripture for specific clarification for every moral doubt that may arise is reasonable. He rejected the idea of the separation of nature and religion. He considered it absurd because he thought both were the same objects to discover the will of God.

Paley concluded that the foundation of humanity's entire system is built around God's almighty will and humanity's rule to be happy. They believe in bringing utilitarianism to stand as a model by retaining that to arrive at God's will concerns any action. He said this "rule is built upon the presumption that God states His general concern is for humanity to obey His will and live by their will to maintain their happiness." [14] He affirmed that the actions of humanity's happiness must be agreeable with God's will and humanity's rule.

He justified this assumption using three propositions of the creation of the human species to determine God's will: First, he said, "God wishes humanity's happiness, or he wishes their misery, or he was indifferent and unconcerned about both." [14] He concluded that God wished their happiness when he provided provision for them. Next, He explained the covenants of God. The outlook that God's provision does promote overall satisfaction. He used the example of adultery, which he determined "would cause the wife to live in purity, causing her to be in want of opportunity or temptation. In turn, deter men from marrying, or render marriage a state of such jealousy and alarm to the husband." [13]

Paley compared Christianity and Utilitarianism. He affirmed that utilitarianism promotes general happiness just as Christianity. His model for "Christian ethics he founded in God to define a motive of the general rule for humanity's happiness." [14] He concluded it is

God's will for humanity to be happy, and society intends to be satisfied too. He asserted that the happiness of society is the same belief of Christianity, and those assumptions of utilitarianism are subservient to the will of God." [14]

Defense of Christianity against Utilitarianism: "Christianity entirely differs from other great faiths in God, not only in the uniqueness of its revelation in Jesus Christ but also in the unique spiritual places in which revelations have launched in human history." [13]

For example, Christianity created a particular type of human character and a specific new social community. Christians established a vast leap looking back from "medieval times that separated it from the great human experience of philosophical, psychological, and humanitarian intellectuals." [11]

On the other hand, the "secularism spirit" [12] shows itself most clearly in the effort to achieve a life filled with personal and social growth that presents non-religious interest rather than loyalty to God. Commitment to God is honoring Him as God. The three characteristics of secularism cannot be conclusive with Christianity. First, secularism shows mediocrity. Mediocrity projects a "fruitage of the secular spirit." [10] The game is to project weakness in a particular objective set as morality but not according to Christianity's standards. The second "fruitage is the aimless pluralism and confusion.

Values: which lost appears even though the secular idols have lost loyalty to God." [10] The third "fruitage of secularism irreligion, it is outwardly so near to religion itself." [10] Yet it is at most the opposite pole, for its interest is selfish, and its effect is to deny that God is God.

CHAPTER V
THE PURPOSES OF PEOPLE BEING ON EARTH

People's thoughts are confronted with a choice to believe, or do not think so, but they cannot make both simultaneously; they must make a choice. Choices can be made with the help of others, by reading books, or just with faith. The essential choice humanity must make is to believe and ask why Christianity is the right path God made society follow through life.

To love God and Obey His Commands: Christianity is a religion of the Western World. Just like any other religion, there are difficulties; truths and lies. In Philippians 2: 12, scripture tells the reader, "continue to work out your salvation with fear and trembling, for it is God who works in you to will and to act according to his good purpose." The purpose of humanity first starts with the partnership with God to triumph in the covenant agreement. Next, humankind's humankind form; Romans 12:2 declared people are formed by renewing their minds, not transformed with self-will. They must get rid of that destructive way of thinking, which determines how they will act.

To be Happy without Harm: Humanism, secularism, and Unitarianism are non-religious thoughts. They see people's purposes formed better when they have the freedom to make their own choices and determine how they will progress. They have developed a system throughout the world to be solely responsible for advancing and expanding cultures through scientific methods. They emphasize humanity's welfare concerning the problems of the world, but without God's Word.

Kingdoms

The Bible reveals two ways to govern people's activities in environments on earth, the Kingdom of the invisible Heaven or the visible governments of civilizations. In the Kingdom of Heaven, the ruling authority is Jesus Christ. He is the Word of God, and the moving force is the Holy Ghost, who is the Spirit of God. In the Kingdom of Heaven, humanity's behaviors are seen as useful, showing God's agape love for one another. Even in the worldwide activities of good, the body of Christ (the church) is to give honor and glory to God, assist with the needs of the trouble, and the life-changing gift of Salvation the Holy Spirits gives to the world.

On the other hand, the governments of civilizations' authority to rule humankind are under Satan's influences, and the moving forces are his army of demons. The scriptures confirm that Lucifer and the falling angel became Prince of the Air and over the earth's activities. His subject's humanity is under his influences on behavior opposite to the mind of Christ. Because of Satan's ruling force in humanity's minds, they seek fleshly desires and perform works that make them look essential. Humanity's concern is trying to discern what God's things are and what the things of Satan are. *Philippians 4:4-9* answers this dilemma.

The Kingdom of God

The Kingdom of God is evident in the Garden of Even; the idea continues with Abraham until John the Baptist; it changed to the Kingdom of Heaven when John introduced the birth, death, and resurrection of Jesus. He proclaimed to return to earth in the power of God to establish the Kingdom of God on earth. Even so, between the great flood of Noah's time and the millennium, these human-made regimes were set up to rule under the guidance of Satan's power, which is indifferent to the Word of God.

Jesus taught in parables about the Kingdom of Heaven as well as the Kingdom of God. In one parable of Jesus taught about the Kingdom of God, He said; that there are many diverse types of fish, but there is only one type of training program to produce one kind of fish in the Kingdom of Heaven. Even so, the door is open for everyone to enter, but on that great awaken day, the door will shut, and all not dressed appropriately for the ceremony will be thrown out into the outer darkness.

Christianity instructs people to make good choices. Humanity based their choices on the righteous thoughts of obeying the way of the Lord. These choices reveal their love for God, themselves, and others. They should live with the hope that their life choices lead them to combat the world's evils and continue to look toward a good life after death. Cited from I Corinthians 12:31 [A2].

On the other hand, it is the belief of "secular humanisms that mature adults are mentally capable of choosing between right and wrong." [13] Mankind can control their life living experiences. Their life choices can produce happiness, prosperity, and success, but their successful lives rely on their ability to manage their minds. The absence of spiritual influences is a significant factor in the way secular humanism lives out life experiences. In other words," secular humanism believes humanity's thoughts are in control of their choices or their life experiences, and they can direct their thoughts and actions at will." [12] They are wrong; the mind's controlling forces are under the control of God or Satan.

The Law of God or Ethics

The will of God is under the rule of this Law and grace. The Law of God sets the stage for what is right and wrong and the fine for doing them. God's things succeed in the ethics of humanity. Ethics are taken from the Law and transformed into civil obedience. The Law of God maintains all, including nature, and all people demanding perfect righteousness and eternal life by works but condemns. By contrast, the Law proceeds God's grace, but the gift of Salvation produces good works that result in faith and righteousness life living. Faith and repentance are always components of Law under the administration of the Holy Spirit. The Law of God in the Bible will never change, but the Spirit is compatible with the Law and gives eternal life to those who accept the gift of Salvation of God.

CHAPTER VI
NEW COVENANT FOR
GOOD LIFE LIVING

In today's society, humanity needs a new kind of protection from evil. Not the safety of following the Law, but that kind is always welcome. A type of spiritual protection from humanity's sins will satisfy the soul and offer insight into humanity's combating evil in their lives. The integration of sin has penetrated into the lifestyles of most cultures. Christianity is an excellent solution against acts of immorality.

First, people need to understand how the covenant agreement of Salvation works in their lives to protect them from the world's wows. The New Covenant was made through Jesus Christ initiated by God made for the universe. The New Covenant God made first with Israel, then with the church, and now given for the world as a whole. God said, "I will put my Law within them, and I will write it on their hearts, and I will be their God, and they shall be my people. No longer shall they teach one another or say to each other. "Know the Lord," for they shall all know me, from the least of them to the greatest, says the Lord; for I will forgive their iniquity, and remember their sin no more."

Cited from Jeremiah 31:31 [A2].

The New Testament is called the New Covenant because Jesus came to this world to die as a sacrificial offering. He came to redeem humankind from Satan's hold on them. Therefore, through Him, humanity has access to God's grace and Salvation to be saved from the hardship of a sinful life. Jesus established a New Covenant. He said, "This cup that is poured out for you is the New Covenant in my blood." Notes: Taken from Luke 22:20 [A2].

The Old Covenant of God was made with the first man Adam. The contract was forfeited when Adam disobeyed God's command and accepted the thoughts of the opposite Words of God. Eve and He agreed with Satan, God's enemy, and because of that agreement, Adam gave over his power to rule this world to Satan. They chose worldly things and decided to live in a different world unprotected against sin rather than live in the economy God prepared for them and the entire world.

Destinies of People after Death

All choices are people's own, and the results of those choices are still their own opinions and their responsibilities. However, their views and commitment can go in the direction of rewards or punishments. A gift is more desirable in comparison to discipline, which is rough treatment. The purpose of God throughout history has been to offer humanity rewards. He rewards good to those who centered their thoughts on the truth of things, on justice, and what is pure. Philippians 4:8 pronounces, "If there is any excellence and if there is anything worthy of praise, think about these things." However, humanity's unfaithfulness and failures were seen in the Law of God's punishments throughout biblical history.

The Laws of God are unchangeable, written before the beginning of time. Even so, the Laws give insight into living right or living wrong. They keep humanity from making unhealthy choices. Society can choose from the two foreordained concepts of living in their minds. Live to honor the Supreme being who created them, believing His words set the course for their lives. Believe Satan's ideology, humankind evolved and is the maker of themselves through reasoning, knowledge, and life experiences, or even live unethically against God's Word.

It is evident, which is the better choice, but Satan's desire for sin entices them to choose the unethical and too harsh way of living. The option is all up to humanity. They cannot say God is the cause of evil, or that he should do something about it. He did at the beginning of time. First, humanity was created after his image to be righteous and holy. Then He gave them the Law to distinguish between right and wrong and to unveil Satan's enticements of desires so they could combat them. Then He sent the Holy Spirit to dwell in humanity to guide and fight the war with the ultimate power of God. Society is without excuse if they neglect such great of Salvation given freely to them.

People on the side of God: The Bible teaches that people choose where they will live afterlife. Their choice of where they will reside after death is based on their works while living on earth. God has offered the gift of Salvation to anyone who will receive it. The gift of Salvation helps him or her to go to heaven. Their good works get them the ticket to enter heaven. When people choose to do God's commands and choose to follow Jesus, Christ teaches they have a better chance to go to heaven.

The Bible teaches that Salvation is a gift to be taken. One of the responsibilities of believers is to instruct people about the love of Christ and the Kingdom of Heaven. It is every Christian's responsibility to tell everyone they meet about the great news; about the Gospel of the Bible those points to the great works of Jesus Christ on Calvary that paid Satan's price to release his control over the minds of humanity.

People are not on the side of God: It is expected not to believe in God or the teachings of Jesus Christ that they will not go to heaven. An unbeliever cannot receive the things of God because he or she cannot see it to claim them. When they disregard God's reality or the teachings of Jesus, they form the ideology of their destiny after death. Most people who believe in secularism believe they should teach others to do good and no harm and be a part of their communities: This principle looks like it belongs to the prophets' golden rule: to love the Lord God with all your heart. Moreover, to do good to your neighbor as you would want them to do good to you. The only thing secularism did not use in brotherly love is to love God with all their hearts.

FINAL REMARKS

 *To conclude, life destinies after death*: People decide which ticket of life they pay to go to heaven or hell the way they live. Should a life of good works pay the ticket to go to hell? On the other hand, the life of self-gratification, a life without keeping the Word of God, a nonethical life, and no input of righteousness is paid to go to heaven.

REFERENCE OF INTRODUCTION OF MAN IN THE WORLD

1. Member of the Emmaus Bible School, *What Christian Believe: Basic Studies in Bible Doctrine and Christian Living*. Chicago, Illinois: Moody Press, 1984, p. 11-12; 47-48. 1951
2. Ryrie, Charles C., *Dispensationalism*, Chicago, Illinois: Moody Press, Pgs. 23-41. 195-197, 1-12, 1966.
3. Erickson, Millard J. *Christology Theology*, Grand Rapids: Baker Books, Pg s. 580-582; 582; 616-617; 606-608; 913. 1999
4. Cherry, Kendra, *The Everything Psychology Book, 2nd Edition*, Avon, Massachusetts: Adams Media, pg. 142. 2010
5. Dake, Finis J. *Dake's Annotated Reference Bible: The New Testament*, Lawrenceville, Georgia, USA, Dake Bible Sales, Inc., pgs. v. 93-4; m 120, pg. 109-4. 1982`
6. Erickson, Millard Christian Theology, Grand Rapids, Michigan: Baker Books, House Company, 1999
7. Scobie, Charlene H.H. *The Ways of Our Lord: An Approach to Biblical Theology*, Grand Rapids Michigan: William B. Eerdmans Publishing Company, p, 475. 2003
8. Ryrie, Charles C. *Basic Theology*, Chicago, Illinois: Moody Press, Pgs. 195-197. 1966
9. Krukonis, Greg and Barr, Tracy, *Evolution for Dummies*: Hoboken, NJ: Wiley
10. Publishing, Inc. pgs. 18.208
11. Richards, Graham. *Human Evolution*: London and New York, Routledge & Kegan Paul, Inc., Pg. 12. 1987
12. Darwin, Charles. *Descent of Man And Selection in Reaction to Sex*, New York, NT: Barnes 7 Noble, Inc. 2004

13. Spain, Richard J. *The Christian Faith & Secularism*: New York, NY & Nashville, Tenn., Abingdon - Cokesbury Press, Pgs. 80-4; 5; 75-76; 77- 6; 74-7
14. Dawkins, Richard. The God Delusion, New York, NY: Houghton Mifflin Company, 2008
15. Thomas, George. Christian Ethics and Moral Philosophy, United States: Charles Scribner's
Sons New York, 1955

INTRODUCTION – MAN IN THE WORD ends

PART I

THE GOD OF THE HOLY BIBLE

CHAPTER I
THE GOD OF CHRISTIANITY

The God of the Holy Bible reigned in two dimensions in history, before the common era and after the common era. In each era, he ruled humanity with different ruling authorities. On the platform of the Old Testament, his ruling power was the covenant of the Law. Still, in the New Testament, His authority or covenant agreements changed to the Holy Spirit, the carrier of the Salvation of God (grace). The birth, life, and death of Jesus Christ moved the time zone from before accession (BC) to after decision (AD).

God of the Old Testament

The Bible starts with "In the beginning God," in the Book of Genesis … and ends with the ending of time, as human beings know of it, in the book of Revelation. The first book of the Old Testament starts with God creating and ends with warnings in Malachi. In Malachi's book, a question-and-answer method is used in stating the argument "*How hast thou loved us?*"

God shows His love when humanity "entreat His flavor, "then He may be gracious to them. The Lord of Host said, "From the rising of the sun to its setting, my name is great among the nations, and in every place, incense is offered to my name, and a pure offering; for my name is great among the nations, but you profane it." The book of Malachi (500-450 B. C.) shows many ways humanity outlawed the flavor of God even being gracious to them for defiance of His covenant agreements. Cited from Malachi 1: 11-12 [A2]

Broken covenant agreements: The Covenant of Levi profaned (Law), causing sin and judgment, not gracious acts of God. The covenant pertained to the altar of worship and offerings. Malachi showed the many ways humanity disrespected God, not honoring and maintaining the altar as a scarce place of prayer. The priest was condemned for corrupting worship and misleading the people; not serving rightfully in worshiping but offering vain offerings to the Lord and not giving seekers accurate instructions causing them to live in iniquity.

The Covenant of Wife and Husband. It was broken because of unfaithfulness to the companion of life caused one's garment of violence; disregarded the union made of the Spirit of life to produce Godly offspring; married daughters of foreign gods.

The Covenant of Life and Peace: It was not honored to show glory to His Great Name in fear and awe; Living in agreement with everyone who does evil, said evil is good; and disregarded blessings of obedience to God of the Old Testament.

The New Testament in Jesus' Name

In the Gospel of St John, the scriptures clarify who is Jesus, "In the beginning was the Word and the Word was with God, and the Word was God. He was at the beginning with God; all things were made through him, and without him was not anything made that was made. In him was life, and the life was the light of men. The light shines in the darkness, and the darkness has not known him." Cited by John 1: 1-5 [A2]

The ministry of Jesus came in two folds. First, He came as God's Word of eternal life and showed he had a special relationship with God. He said his teaching is not His, but God's. He said, "If any man does His will, he will know whether the teaching is from God or whether he spoke of His authority." (John 7:17-18) He spoke with the authority of God and the power of God when he performed signs of miracles, changed the water into wine, healed the blind man, and raised the dead. He taught about the Salvation of God He offered to anyone who would believe He is the Son of God.

Jesus cried out and said, "He who believes in me believes not in me, however, for Him who sent me. Moreover, he who sees Me sees Him who sent me. Jesus, came as the light of the world, that whoever believes in me may not remain in darkness. If anyone hears my saying and does not keep them, I do not judge him, for I did not come to judge the world, however, to save the world. He who rejects me and does not receive my sayings has a judge; the Word I have spoken will be his judge on the last day. For I have not spoken on my authority, the Father who sent me has Himself given me commandment what to say and what to speak. In addition, I know that His commandment is eternal life. What I say, therefore, I say as the Father has bidden me." Cited by John 12: 44-50 [A2]

In the other ministry of Jesus, He came to be a sacrifice to take away humanity's sins. John the Baptist saw him and said, "Behold, the Lamb of God. Who takes away the sin of the world! " (John 1: 29) Jesus testified on many occasions proclaiming the work He is doing the Father had sent Him to do. Jesus declared his ministry, saying, "I am the living bread that came down from heaven; if anyone eats of this bread, he will live forever; and bread which I shall give for the life of the world is my flesh." Cited from John 6:48-51 [A2].

On another occasion, he spoke these words. He lifted his eyes to heaven and said, "Father, the hour has come; glorify thy Son that the one may glorify thee; since thou hast given him power over all flesh, to give eternal life to all whom thou have given him. Moreover, this is eternal life that they know thee the only true God and Jesus Christ, whom thou hast sent. I glorified thee on earth, having accomplished the work, which thou gave me to do; and now, Father, glorify thou me in thy presence with the glory, which I had with thee before the world was made. Cited from John 17: 1-7 [A2]

CHAPTER II
THE IMAGE OF GOD

Today, the great argument about humanity's identity is about who they are and how they should act. The Bible gives the picture that man created in God's image should look and act like Him. For some people, human beings made are after the exact physical copy of God, but for others, this means the way they think is the same as God. Even so, the problem is humankind does not look or think like God.

The controversy over this argument is how humanity looks and acts do not represent God's image or likeness. The word image means a duplicate or a copy, and this idea is hard to apply to man being an exact copy of God. Therefore, to determine if the man is a copy of God, examining God's religions and followers needed to take place. Still, most faiths and followers of God do not follow the signature or the definition of what God is like or how He acts. So, to simplify and shorten this argument, the purpose of God's signature is "the Supreme Being, the creator, and ruler of the universe, [A1] whom no one has ever seen.

The word image of God showed up many times in the books of the Bible. The first one in Genesis pointed to God creating "man in their image to have dominion over the fish of the sea, and over the birds of the air, and over the cattle, and over all the earth, and over every creeping thing that creeps upon the earth … and be fruitful and multiply." The scriptures (Genesis 1: 26-28) revealed that God made all the rest of His creation different from humanity, and humanity is superior to all other creatures. It is not the physical likeness of God, or His acts stated in verses, but humankind's ways and their resemblance to rule the earth as God. Cited from Genesis Chapter One [A2]

The word likeness used in Genesis 5: 1-3 gives the picture again that God created the people of their similarity and gave them names. He named a male, a man, and a female, a woman. God created the man from the dust of the earth and breathed life into him, but he took a rib from the man's side and made it into a woman. Their makeup continued when they started producing offspring in their likeness and called the first a male child because he would grow into a man. Cited from Genesis Chapter Two [A2]

Then the Lord God said, "Behold, the man has become like one of us in knowing good and evil. Now, lest he put forth his hand and also take of the tree of life and eat and live forever. The Bible explains the first woman and man disobeyed God and inherited a sinful nature. A sinful nature is the opposite of the nature of God. In this scripture, God's image portrays people as God because they now know the difference between good and evil. Cited from Genesis 3:22 [A2]

Leaving the Old Testament and Accepting the New

Those who live in the natural body do not know how to live spiritually. The assumption or possibility of humanity could learn to live spiritually with a carnal mind is none. They need to put off the old self, which belongs to the "former manner of life and is corrupted through deceitful desires. Then they would be renewed in the spirit of their minds, and put on the new nature, created after the likeness of God in true righteousness and holiness." Cited from Ephesians 4:20-24 [A2]

The sinful nature of humanity or "the nature of man does not comprehend the things of the Spirit of God." They cannot accept them because they are folly to them, and they are unable to understand them because they are spiritually discerned." When humanity takes their state of living in a sinful nature seriously, they will call upon God to help them see they need to change from living in a sinful nature to living in a spiritual one; humanity can confess they resemble God's image when acting like Him. Cited from 1 Corinthians 2:14 [A2]

Living in the image of God as believers of Christ: The concept of humanity living in God's image is based on foreknowing to predestined and conformed to His Son's image. Humanity transformation happens after their verification is accepted by God to be the firstborn among many brothers. Moreover, those whom he predestined also called, and those whom he called he also justified, and those whom he justified he also glorified. Cited from Romans 6:6 [A2]

The believer who accepts Jesus Christ is transferred from the old person into the new one. They know their "old selves were crucified with him so that the body of sin might be brought to nothing so that they would no longer be enslaved to sin." The first human (Adam) beings the cause of God's separation happen because of disobedience, and the second man (Jesus) rejoined humanity to be accepted in the beloved. Cited from Romans 8:29-30 [A2]

The appeal to humanity by the mercies of God is "to present their bodies as a living sacrifice, holy and acceptable to God, which is their spiritual worship. They are not to be conformed to this world, but be transformed by the renewal of their minds, that by assessing them may discern what the will of God is, what is good, acceptable, and perfect." When humanity presents their bodies as living sacrifices, they act and show God's likeness. Cited from Romans 12:1-2 [A2]

The old person transferred into the new man when he accepts Jesus Christ as his personal Lord and Savior. Holy living is the process that makes the change. The nature man takes on God's image when he or she learns and lives how the Bible teaches life living should be lived. Then the scripture becomes a reality in the life of the believer that he or she "must be perfect; as their heavenly Father is, perfect." Cited from Matthew 5:48 [A2]

God's concepts: Just who is God, what makes Him God, and should He be worshiped? Most religions teach they worship the one true God, especially Christianity, Judaism, and Islam. They believe He is the creator of all things. His ultimate powerful force is seen in the elements of nature. His presence is eternal, starts from the beginning, and never ends. God is God, Yahweh, and Allah (and other names) because of His definition, characteristics, and personages say so. He is God to be worshiped.

This section aims to see what makes God - God. As the Supreme Being, the characteristic of God has to be omnipotent, omnipresent, and omniscient. His sovereignty is displayed throughout the earth and the universe. He is the Father of humanity, the fighter against evil, and the life-sustainer of all existence, including nature. The definition of God makes it impossible for others to say they are God.

The Titles of God

The titles of God are universal and fall under many definitions and purposes. The sorting of God is impossible. This or that has possibilities because His name ranked as the creator and sustainer of all life on earth. He maintains the life, beauty, and functions of the inhabitation and nature. Even so, God's one identity is He is the Supreme Spirit Being who created the universe, earth, and life on earth. His universal name is God and worshiped in the thoughts of all human minds. Archaeologists, historians, and theologians have found temples to signify He is worth worshiping throughout history.

Definition: God's concept is admired as the one creator, sustainer of life and the universe, and nature maintainer. He is God because of His supreme natural ability to do things that no other human being or anything else can do.

Characteristics: God's attributes of love are active in human feelings too. Agape love tops all other love. It shows the love of God not according to the love of man, but the love of God that is the root of goodness. Agape is the highest form of love. Agape love is a supreme and excellent type of love that is unconditional love. This love will obey every Word that proceeds out of the mouth of God.

His Personages: The Trinity reveals the personages of God. The three forms of God are the Father, the sustainer of lives, the Son who creates life, and the Holy Spirit who empowers life into existence. They are single in identity, but they are one in the body. No part of Trinity will work without the other, but each has its own identity and purposes.

God is a universal God. His name, attributes, and Law are acknowledged worldwide. All cultures see Him as the Almighty Supreme Spirit Being that deserves to be worshiped in giving. He is seen as the Most Gracious, the Most Merciful, and the Law that shows His being. There are many interpretations of God and many ways to serve Him, but the reality is what makes Him God and that He is personal to each person.

CHAPTER III
WHAT MAKES GOD
THE ONE TRUE GOD

God is defined as the Supreme Being that created humanity. He created all things. The three characters of God make Him God: He is omnipotence, omnipresent, and omniscient. Without these capabilities, God could not be God, and He could not have the power to rule His creation.

The Characteristics of God

First, the omnipotent characteristic of Him proves He is of great power. As the Supreme Being, He can do just what he says he will do. His forces, seen as the powerful forces of nature, are examples of His power. Being omnipotent, His power is infinite or limitless because of His Word's ability to affirm His actions. The Word of God is one of a kind because His creation will never be erased. His Word is incapable of replacement with another. The Word of God is part of the personage of the three.

Second, God is omnipresent, allowing His presence to be everywhere because He is Spirit. Through the beginning of time and the ending of time, He is the God of biblical history in all cultures. He is the infinite Spirit of the universe. The name of the universal God is in all religions. The word of God represents His very presence in human history.

Third, God has the characteristic of omniscience, an all-knowing God. God knows all in the lives of people because He created them. God's knowledge about them gives him the edge to predict their future, see their needs, and understand and know the outcome of their choices in life. He has the knowledge and ability to maintain the world and take care of its inhabitants at the time. His all-knowing capabilities create His personages of the Trinity. God sits on the high seat of His authority, ruling as God in the capacity of the Father, the Son, and the Holy Spirit.

Trinity

God is the three capacities of the Trinity. The Holy Spirit carries the Salvation of God's promises to give the world the faith they need to sustain their worries and meet their needs. His Son creates all existence of this world and has the power to change them at will. The Father looks through the entire world to locate one of His children in need to give them a blessing. The commands of God provide humanity protection from the evil thoughts of this world. The covenants of God are the agreements with Him that He will do as He has promised. His commands are set in action to safeguard the planet.

The supreme being: On earth, all people understand God as the Supreme Spirit Being. Three seeable avenues link the concept of the reality of God. One way God discerned is through nature. Nature displays God's powers and glory. Second, a revealed revelation about Him formulates between him and the perceiver. Third, God is one of a kind, and If humankind tries to work in His compactly, they will show zero accountability.

The God of Nature

The God of nature produces water on earth which is another necessity for the survival of humankind. Earth masses are made of "71% water." [5] "An "adult human body comprises 60% of water; the brain and heart are composed of 73% water, and the lungs are about 83% water. The skin contains 64% water, muscles and kidneys are 79%, and even the bones consist of too, which consists of 31% water." [5] Moreover, water is used for all of the needs of humankind. Without water, humanity cannot survive on earth. Hence, without the rain that the clouds make, humanity could not live on earth. Water is the spring of life that makes life possible.

The God of nature makes food, too. That is another necessity of humankind's need for survival. The earth produces enough vegetation, sea habitations, and animals used as food to feed people. So again, without the food that the God of nature provides, humankind could not survive here on earth! The natural elements of the world humanity use to support their existence. Therefore, without these natural elements that come from the land, people could not exist here on earth.

Secondly, God's power and glory are shown in nature when the forces of nature work His handiwork of beauty or display the powerful destructive forces in the world. There are many arguments about if God has control over nature or if the character is a natural phenomenon. The God of nature mighty acts because of the natural forces of the earth's elements and the universe. Still, it is undeniable that the God of nature does show powers over nature that humankind has not created or cannot control. Yes, it is the power of the God of nature, but God's creation displays such powers and wonders of the earth's mystical forces and the universe under His Laws of nature.

Another natural display of God's glory is the beautification of the earth, the universe, and its habitations. The oceans, the land, and the water that covers this great earth are breathtaking. Man cannot put together the elements or the design to create such wonders. Throughout the planet, God's handiwork is seen, but what makes these beautiful sights so great for humanity is that they can see living-color schemes. God created people to see His great enterprise in living color.

The colors in the universe and earth show their ability to change, become bright, and the ark, and display various beautiful designs. For example, humanity represents many colors; in particular, their many different skin shades of color represent their nature locale. People who are dark-skinned live below the equator line of earth and people with lighter skin tone live above it in the appropriate way of their living zones.

Nature has other ways that reveal the concept of God. His character displays His divine natural powers of earth, shown in all of God's creations, in His name, and His sovereignty. In the Letter of

Paul to the Romans, he wrote, "Ever since the creation of the world his eternal power and divine nature, invisible though they are, have been understood and seen through the things he has made. So, they are without excuse." Cited from Romans 1:20 [A2]

The earth is one display of the creations of God. His creation of the land and universe is to support the existence of earth's habitations. It proves the creation of the world, and the universe was exclusive to help humanity's continued life and habitation. The design of the planet and the universe is another proof of the existence of God. Nature continually shows the power and ability of God. Nature tells the story of life. It continues to exist through turmoil, and the sun, moon, and elements continue to function to provide an environment for humankind to live in.

God of Creation: Christianity gives one version of the order of creation, but there are others. In most cases, there is a supreme being that creates. A great definition of the God of creation is omnipotent. There is no other who can be called the almighty, the all-powerful, or the unstoppable. He is the founder of the universe, earth, and all life substances.

The God of Revelations: In the Old Testament, God governed the world of people under the Law's guidance, the Ten Commandments. However, in the New Testament, Jesus says he "did not come to change the Law but to full fill it." The Old Testament tells of the change that would take place in the New Testament. God said he would do a new thing on the earth; he would change humankind's hearts to serve Him, which is the Holy Ghost's job. Cited from Matthew 5:17 [A2]

Jesus came to His people of the Hebrew race to tell them what God expected of them. He wanted them to believe and to act in a holy, righteous way that represents God. Jesus visited many of their towns' preaching in the synagogues, healing the sick, and teaching His twelve disciples the ways of God. On most occasions, in the cities He visited, the people did not believe in His messages. Their disbelief of Jesus being the Son of God opened the way for the gentiles to receive the great Salvation, the gift of the Holy Spirit, He said He would send back after he rose from being dead.

The second concept is a revelation about God. A revelation is an idea of existence or a close encounter with Him. Revelations usually materialize in dreams, or the revelation of His presence comes from the "consciousness of an experience" [6] of people. Disclosures are resolved from the sense of the reality of that experience. The concept of the knowledge of God is from the Bible or other sources. A revolution assumes God's existence. Even though everyone has an idea of God, making it impossible to prove His non-existence, making it impossible to deny that He exists.

Another characteristic of God is the divine. Divine gives a picture of what God is like being God. As a divine God, He holds the state of things that come from His supernatural power or deity. The holy things are scarce and divine. The divinity of God wrapped around His sovereignty of Being. He is the dominant of all forces, all controls, and all authorities.

Trinity is the three personages of God, but it can be considered a characteristic of Him. These characteristics of him are the three attributes: He creates; He is all-good. Moreover, humanity acknowledges, that God is everything, and because He is everything, He sustains all things.

The two mythologies of the concept/meaning of God come from August Hopkins and Thomas Aquinas. In his book the August Hopkins Strong Systematic Theology, he established God's existence on some type of basis that most knowledge of humans provides proof or rational thought, "all knowledge depends on Him" [1]. On the other hand, Thomas Aquinas considered the meaning of God realized through "movement /exchange." [2]

Aquinas's observation of the fivefold proof that shows God's existence is the proof of movement and exchange. The argument for motion appeals to human senses. Humans' minds can perceive certain things on the earth, such as the universe being in motion. The assumption of the theory of action is whatever is in motion must be put in motion by another, but this push of the movement needs another sign to push it, then another into action; that could continue for eternity. Therefore, it is necessary to arrive at a first mover to be the eternal God that put the first movement in motion.

Next, Aquinas used the theory of efficient cause to prove the existence of God through observation. Observations of people's senses reveal that there is an order of efficient causes. "The ordering process has to be the efficient cause of another. All efficient causes follow in order, the first is the cause of the intermediate cause, and the intermediate is the second cause of the ultimate cause. There has to be the initiation of the first cause to put in effect the second and so forth." [2] Therefore, the first initiation cause is assigned to the efficient cause of God.

The third proof of Aquinas showed evidence of God's existence using nature. He said what makes God's existence consider the possibility and necessity centers on the natural presence of things and is not likely to be seen. If everything is not expected to be, then at one time, there could have been nothing in existence. The truth would show nothing in reality because that which does not exist only begins to exist by something already existing. This is the concept of the existence of God.

Aquinas' fourth concept of the existence of God comes from the gradation found in things. Now the maximum in any genus is the cause of all in that genus; as fire, which is the maximum heat, is the cause of all hot things. Therefore, there must also be something that is identified to all beings as the cause of their being, goodness, and every other perfection; and this we call God.

Finally, Aquinas' used his proof of God's existence in the natural things in the universe and the world to show its governance theory. The theory states that some things stand on their intelligentsia senses, and others have none. They lack intelligence, such as natural bodies, which act for an end, which is evident from their acting always, or always, in the same way. They pretend to obtain or to achieve their given results. Now whatever lacks intelligence cannot move towards its purposeful end. Their inability to move forward in power and knowledge, but with "God has pre-authorized intelligentsia design; they move to their results." [3] Therefore, the idea is that an intelligent being moves them to the end of their purpose.

To Know God is to Understand Him: Most theologians agree that knowing the meaning of God or understanding the concept only comes through revelations. They declare that humankind can only get to know God is only if He reveals Himself to them. A revelation experience is a model for understanding the meaning of God based on the human experience. People experience God when a revelation about Him is revealed to them. Revelation also means disclosure, a "theological concept that means divine disclosure." [4]

The Only God

People fear God because He is powerful. His power is displayed within the laws of nature. God has already set all things into existence, and the rules of nature move according to His predestined decree. As the Superior Being, in most cultures, they see Him in total control of time, the destiny of this world, and their lives. Even though most cultures attracted the woes of life to the concept of evil; on the other hand, natural disasters are harsh, under the acts of God, but under the control of the laws of nature.

God is invisible and visible in the lives of His creation. He lives in the minds of people and communicates with them through words. He is the creator of stories, and he gave humanity the responsibility to name all existence according to their likeness. He is also unseen. The powerful forces of nature make it possible to reveal His powers behind His strengths. No other can perform such powerful movements of nature as God.

However, God governs humanity according to His promises, Laws, and grace. God's promises set in action are because of His Word and covenant agreements. The Law of God is His nature and cannot be substituted.

His Promises: The Promises of God are His covenant agreements. God will honor every one of His promises, but if His Law is broken then the decree executes judgement.

His Laws: Outcomes of nature and people's actions judged are according to good and evil rules, that is, the Laws of God. Genesis tells of Adam and Eve's story when they took the fruit from the tree of good and evil knowledge. God told them now that they knew both sides of the influences of their experience, they had become like

Gods knowing good and evil, and their performance would be the same.

His Grace: Being pardoned for disobedience is the grace of God. It is His mercies renewed each morning. Great is His faithfulness. When does His grace cease to exist? God's grace is a part of Him; it is eternal like Him.

CHAPTER IV
THE EXCELLENCY OF GOD

Most religions tell of the excellency of God expressed in several ways. For example, the greatness of God is displaced by Christians in the use of His power, in their use of His glory, and when they use His knowledge. Christianity tells of God's excellency from Psalms and Proverbs' readings in the Old Testament (the Tora) of the Holy Bible.

The most excellent is His Spirit.

In the New Testament, Peter speaks about a transformed life, and Jesus touched the hand of a young girl that came back to life. A life change can be seen as a transformed life of becoming godly or a transfer from a life coming back from the dead. For example, God's Power consists of His ability to give new life and bring back life after death.

Theories of worship: God brings knowledge, peace, assurance, and safety to the thoughts of humankind. God is the Great Teacher, Provider, and Protector in most cultures. Most cultures practice ways to gain their religious rights. Others perform rituals or practices that they believe will influence God to receive his benefits or blessings from Him. Still, others think there is just one way to live and worship God to accept the things of God. However, Christianity proposes an excellent way of honoring God.

The Aboding Place of God: The Scripture puts God in a high dwelling place. For example, Psalm 24 gives the scenario humankind must have clean hands and a pure heart to reach God in his abiding place. God dwells everywhere, for the Lord God we serve is omnipresent; He lives and breathes in all things. God is presence does not present in temples or shrines, but the Holy Spirit moves like the breath of the wind.

The Scripture puts God in a high-dwelling place. For example, Psalm 24 gives the scenario humankind must have clean hands and a pure heart to reach God in his abiding place. God dwells everywhere, for the Lord God we serve is omnipresent; He lives and breathes in all things. The presence of God dwells on earth, not in temples or shrines, but in the Holy Spirit who moves like the breath of the winds.

Moreover, man's origin comes from the earth, universe, and all living things created by God. God exists within all living, and none living matter because he is the source of all beings. God portrayed is as the great creator, the all-knowing, and all-loving within the religious sects. Humans cannot see God, but they only believe he exists, and therefore one must act on what they believe. The theory of God living is He is where all sources of life and usefulness live.

Abraham Maslow said man's self-actualization causes him to be fair, but what about the problem of evil? The issue of good and evil is a mental projection of the mind that speaks to humankind's physical feelings. The idea of good and evil establishes an underlying standard of right or wrong. Humanity has a built-in system of understanding good and evil and the ability to choose right or wrong.

The Belief System in God

First deism is the belief in a creator who made the world but did not take a personal interest in it -- it does not require worship, answer prayers, judge behavior, or necessarily promise life after death. Deism is a benign belief because there are no consequences for accepting or rejecting it. The type of influence this belief system has on man believes God is not acting as a Father. He does not work on their behalf or does not connect with them or give them protection or gifts.

On the other hand, deism means belief in the existence of a supreme being, specifically of a creator who does not intervene in the universe. The term was used chiefly during the intellectual movement of the 17th and 18th centuries. The idea accepted a creator's existence based on reason but rejected belief in a supernatural deity who interacts with humankind. Deism is different from Christian deism. Deism is opposed to the doctrine of predestination in which everything that happens is according to the will of God, but instead, tends to believe in the concept of free will.

Second, there is theism, which is the belief in an active, officious God who not only created the world (and some believe fine-tuned it for human use). They may also require worship, answer prayers, judge sinners, and have created a divine Son or other entities to live among humans. Most theists are 100 percent certain their god(s) exist and have faith in this without any objective, verifiable evidence. There are many theistic religions, each of which insists it is the only true one.

Atheism is the absence of belief in any gods. They believe in no God. The definition of Atheism is "one who has recognized that she or he sincerely has no belief in any gods." [A1] That definition covers all atheists plus agnostics who say they do not believe. The belief there is no God is a belief system, and it is not a religion. They build their premise on there is no evidence there is God. They reject the assertion that there are gods. Atheism is not a religion or belief system. Nor does it assert disbelief in gods or a denial of gods. Others in America are atheists when they call themselves humanists, freethinkers, or even cultural Catholics.

Nevertheless, they are open to the slight possibility they could be wrong and willing to accept the existence of god(s) if clear, objective, verifiable evidence was to appear. Therefore, they do not have faith in the nonexistence of god(s). They simply have no belief in any gods.

Materialism considers material possessions and physical comfort more important than spiritual values. The ideology of materialism is an incredibly pervasive philosophy that asserts that nothing exists beyond the material universe, which is composed of matter and energy, the idea described by Albert Eisenstein was not necessarily a materialist. Materialism is the doctrine that nothing exists except matter and its movements and modifications.

Lastly, agnosticism is formal uncertainty about the existence or nonexistence of god(s). The agnostic asserts it is impossible to prove either the existence or the nonexistence of deities. Theists sometimes try to tell atheists that they are agnostics because they cannot prove God's existence. This is not true. An atheist has no belief in any god(s). That is different from believing it is impossible to tell if God exists or not.

Theism, Deism, Atheism, and Materialism: Theories of "theism, deism, and atheism" are terms that tell different accounts about God; how people see Him, how they relate to Him, and experience God. The experience of God is according to their faith. The word Thesis means belief in one God as creator and ruler of all things, without rejection of evolution. Theists affirmed that an entirely conscious understanding of being, or mind, existing from eternity was the cause of all other things.

God should have the features; of a God-like Father, a God-like Son, and a God-like Spirit. These God-like attributes are called the Trinity, according to the Christian faith. The Trinity's titles are to interconnect with humankind as the Father, the Son, and the Spirit. Humanity fine these three facets or beings like God from a religious point of view. He can be a father, a son, and a spirit too, but all are different from God's because the design is for humans. God's characteristics are created and designed for Him and are used to express His caregiving nature to humanity. Notes: Taken from Frederick Carl Eiselen, Edwin Lewis, and David G. Downey, in their book The Abingdon Bible Commentary (1929)

The material God is in another window other than biblical. They look for an exchange of happiness. Jesus said His kingdom was not of this world, and believers are traveling through looking for a building whose builder and maker is God. On the other hand, materialist sees the message of Jesus as giving up all this and getting what?

The message of Jesus used is in Mathew 10:28-31. Jesus said, "Truly, I say to you, there is no one who has left house or siblings, mother, father, children, or land, for my sake besides, for the gospel, who will not receive a hundredfold now in this time, houses, children, and lands, with persecutions and in the age to come eternal life. But many that are first will be last, and the last first."

Materialists used Mark 10:29-31 to explain, "What happiness do you promise us in exchange." [8] They have three periods to support their response. First in view are eschatology and the coming kingdom. They should leave the social system for His sake. They said it imposes his liberating ministry to preach this exchange. Next, "From this time forward, this break will continue being about a hundred-fold fruition of everything left behind except for the father, doubtless because it is "only the father" (cf. Matt.23:9). Third, look for the kingdom of God where it is eternal life. They say Jesus 'message sent a message of happiness, but they are wrong. Jesus' message is a warning of this world's things are nothing to desires in comparison to the things that will come.

CHAPTER V
ARGUMENTS FOR THE
EXISTENCE OF GOD

The label or name for God is God. God's title is a universal language, and the belief of His existence is true in most cultures. Most cultures used a universal language about God's presence throughout the world, but all see Him in different fashions. Theism argues there are different approaches to how humanity should prove the existence of God. For example, Christian theologians and Christian philosophes disagree on how the truth of God's presence is confirmed and the facts about Him should be revealed. Both believe without faith, and it is impossible to believe in the presence of God. However, one approach thinks the reality of God is the beginning of religion. This type of trust is based on revelation and demonstration of beliefs and based on the source of its reasoning. The other approach sees God's existence in the articles of faith that contain truths that cannot be proven. They stilled by fact, not by reason alone. They hold the presupposed truths of the preambles of the existence of God.

The "transcendental arguments" of the presence of God proclaims, "all human experience and action is proof of the existence of God." "God's existence is the necessary condition of their intelligibility." [4] Secondly, the "logical and philosophical arguments" [10] for or against God's existence missed the point altogether. They did not point to an all-monotheistic God, or henotheistic see as the perfect being. This idea of; or against God cancels out the possibility that he exists at all.

On the Deity of God or Many: There are so many names for God, many ways to worship Him, and many distinct types of followers of God. As stated above, God's image does represent anything according to man's theory of what God is. This belief in the character of God has enlightened man's imagination. There are additions and subtractions to the idea of the makeup of God. One theory of man sees God as an individual, and another view sees Him as a God of many, and even there is the absence of God or a God of many faces. There are three faces of God. First, one God, or the God of many, or even the God of many faces.

The beliefs in monotheistic God worshipers believe they worship the only true God. Today, there are three major monotheistic religions in the western world. Even though they started in Africa, all three have migrated to the western and eastern continents. Their teachings have stayed the same throughout history but with some minor alternations.

On the continent of North America, in Europe, and throughout the world, Christian believers believe that their god is the God that needed to come from heaven to restore humanity from their sins. God appeared on earth as Jesus to teach humankind how to live and worship God. This teaching strategy is from the Holy Bible. They believe in the Trinity: God the Father, God the Son, and God the Holy Spirit. Jesus is the Son of God, who came into the world to save the world from their sins. When a person accepts that He is their savior, is Baptist in water, and receives the Holy Spirit, they can then experience a relationship with Jesus, the Holy Spirit, and God.

Judaism expresses they encountered God and gave their prophet Moses the Ten Commandments. They say they are the chosen representative of God, and through them, God blesses the rest of the world. Israel's historical story tells of their bondage, their experiences as they travel through the wilderness, and how God delivered them and promise them covenants and promises written in the Old Testaments but fulfilled in the New Testament.

Islamic faith believers should have faith in Allah, and His prophet is Mohmand. The majority of Islamic faith believers still are located on Africa's continent, but they have migrated worldwide. This religion has a primary teaching strategy that it is without a doubt that conformity is justifiable if Allah is God. They teach from the Holy Koran.

Henotheistic God: The God of many of gods with many faces is faith in a henotheistic faith God. These religious are located mostly on the eastern continents of the world. The three most commonly held beliefs of this faith are Buddhism, Hinduism, and Confucius. There are many types of Asians' confidence, and their religious teachings differ from each other. This faith believes in the power of change or the ability to be great lies within oneself.

Atheism: The argument about God's existence for an atheist is there is not enough sufficient evidence that proves there is a reason to believe that any God exists. They say that God's nature reality experience is in the mind, and that is not a natural reality because the experience is in the sense of that believer. Atheism has many beliefs about the nonexistence of God.

For example, a *positive atheist* asserts that no deities exist. On the other hand, cynical atheist declares they do not believe in God's existence but claim there is a possibility "there to be none." A *weak agnostic* will say the existence or nonexistence of deities is unknown. They are knowable. On the other hand, a *strong agnostic* claims that humans cannot know but are not necessarily unknowable. Agnosticism does not define a belief or disbelief in God. Notes: taken from [A1]

The Christian Bible's God's revelation: The Holy Bible of the Christianity faith is about God and His creation. The division of the book is two pains. The first part of the book is the Old Testament and derived from Hebrew descent, which tells of their relationship with God. The name of this book is Tora. The second part of the book is called the New Testament; the book tells of the fulfillment of the Old Testament's prophecies, namely about the birth and the works of Jesus Christ. The Epistles, written by Jesus' Disciples, are vital to the understanding of the Salvation of God.

Within the testaments' books, there are also books telling different themes in different settings and times. The first book of the Old Testament is Genesis starts with the story of creation. Genesis gives an account of the beginning of time was created by God. (Genesis 1:1). There are three Superior Beings who took part in creation: God, the Holy Spirit (God's Spirit), and the Word (Jesus). The three supernatural beings are the Trinity and will always be the major players in the Bible. They played separate roles but are all considered as one united entity of three personages.

Revelations: Christians affirm no one can see God, and the only way humanity can get to know Him, only if he reveals Himself. The revelation of God is about the things of God, but mostly about Him. They speak about individuals empowered with a supernatural power that gives them the ability to experience and see spiritual things they would not have experienced or seen in reality.

These supernatural things did materialize and were visible or were already present here on earth. People have reported revelations of God; and other supernatural being such as angels, demons, and other visual spiritual beings here on earth. Besides, Christian believers believe they have been empowered to perform metaphysical healing on the sick and have the power to cast out unwanted demonic spirits, which they believe influence the human thoughts that are causes of their unwanted negative behavior.

God is a belief in the human mind. He is not seen on earth as other things materialized or seen as men, such as birds flying in the sky. He does not physically exist, but He does live spiritually in people's thoughts and transforms into their reality as the ultimate spiritual being. He is like the wind that blows in the air. His present does not matter like seen on earth. The thought of God materializing and seeing on earth is unthinkable or unlikeable. Although, there have been reports of other spiritual beings such as angels and demons on the ground. People have reported events like this daily.

Even so, there are recorded events in the Old Testament that people confessed, such as mighty men of God had the opportunity to get a glimpse of God here on earth. The prophet Moses reveals he saw "the back of God passing through the cliff of the mountain." Other revelations of the appearance of supernatural things people reported they experience them in dreams, meditation, and when in trances. Cited from Exodus 33: 17-23 [A2]

Most cultures' concept of God varies because God materializes in the thought of people differently. Therefore, God is seen as, understood as, viewed as, and worshiped as God of many ways and fashions. Some religious leaders and laypeople believe they can speak to

God directly, and they think He has given them supernatural power to heal the sick, and they can perform miracles. (Events contrary to laws of nature) They see and experience God in diverse ways.

Most theologians agree that knowing the meaning of God or understanding that God is revealed only through revelations. They declared that humankind could only get to know God is only if He revealed Himself to them. Theologians usually affirm four ways God shows Himself through revelations. They are called the "*Models of Revelation.*" [6] The modes of revelations are a revelation as doctrine, revelation as presence; revelation as experience; and revelation as history. Correctly understood, they represent different emphases within the Christian understanding of revelations.

Revelations as doctrine: This approach shows characteristics of conservative evangelical and catholic neo-scholastic schools and, in modified or supplement forms, continues to exercise considerable influence within the Christian tradition of the church's doctrine, instead of the traditional philosophy format.

Revelation as knowing His presence: The most important statement of this approach is Emil Brunner's Truth as the Encounter, which sets out the idea of a revelation as a personal communication of God – that is to say, a Communication or impartation of the personal presence Of God within the believer. The lordship and love of God communicate in no other way than by God is self-giving. Brunner based his idea on Martin Buber's analysis of "I-Thou," and "I-Tt" [6] relations insist that there is a relational element to revelation.

Brunner's point is that God does not merely convey information in the process of revelation. Revelation concerns the conveying of God's presence, rather than mere details concerning God. Brunner's concept of truth as encounter conveys the two elements of what he regards as a correct indulgence of revelation. It is historical and personal.

Revelation as an experience: The revelation experience is a model based on the human experience. God understood through the experience of an individual. This approach widely held is associated with German liberal Protestantism in the nineteenth century, especially F. D. F. Schleiermacher and A. B. Ritschl. Schleiermacher's background of Moravian Pietism. Moravian Pietism emphasized a personal devotion to Christ and the importance of emotional awareness of conversion. In the book *"Christian Faith*, Schleiermacher emphasizes the Christian faith is not primarily conceptual."* [6] Still, doctrines are to be seen as second-order jargons of its primary religious truth, which is the experience of redemption.

Revelation in history: According to German theologian Wolfhart Pannenberg, Christian theology's theme centers on revelation as history. "Christian theology is based upon analysis of universal and accessible in history, rather than inward subjectivity of personal human existence or a particular interpretation of that history." [6] For Pannenberg, a revelation is an event that is recognized and interpreted as an active act of God.

The revelation of God revealed, "Revelation means disclosure." [6] It is considered a theological concept, which means divine exposure. The Jews recorded Yahweh's (God's directions) to them in the Torah and commentaries recorded in Exodus's Book. The Old Testament's incredible event in which God liberated an unorganized enslaved people from the mightiest power of the age reveals most of Him in revelation form.

The Influences of God: Usually, God or the Supreme being in the Old Testament will communicate with one individual called a prophet or called a man of God who, in return, relays messages to a particular group of people. For example, the tribes of Israelites, a Hebrew race of people, believed God contacted them through the prophet Moses. God commissioned moses to bring them out from under the bondage of Pharaoh's rule over them. Israel's children experienced the wilderness where they could communicate with God, and He could share with the Hebrews to inform the world about who He is and what He expects of humanity. Notes: taken from Stibbs, pg. 11)

The authors, Esposito, Darrell J. Fasching, and Todd Lewis gave a brief synopsis of their theory about God's likeness in their book *World Religions Today* (2009). The above quote uses the aphorism Lord of Host, which means God. There are many so-called ideals, versions, and representations of God. Man sees God in many dimensions. God's statues represented a spirit, a man, an animal, or even he can be a statue in the eyes of man.

However, in most cases, cultures or religions see God as the ultimate powerful spiritual entity that can communicate with the human race. He is the maximum power of nature in the universe. He is the One God among many races with many appellations and performances. The problem with God of many faces pointing to the true God. Christianity declares they found Him.

As the magisterium, the church is the term for the deposit of revelation or the promise of God's real meaning. The church's accumulated insights over the years have employed such contexts. According to this approach, disclosure is primarily in propositional form. This approach regards disclosure as taking the form of doctrinal statements that are set forth by the church. The messages found are in both scripture and unwritten traditions. Notes: taken from McGrath, pg. 202-203

This approach was severely criticized by the post-liberal theologian such as George Lindbeck in his book "*Nature of Doctrine.*" Lindbeck argued the policy rejected was the intellectualist and literalist. It was resting on the mistaken assumption that it is possible to state God's objective as truth. Notes: taken from McGrath, pg. 205

Faith Statement: A doctrinal faith statement is what the church believes. It starts with the I or we statement. For example, the Eastern University doctrinal statement begins with our belief that the Bible, composed of the Old and New Testaments, is inspired by God, and serves as the rule of faith and practice, being the authoritative witness to God's truth embodied in Jesus. [9]

The Puzzling Appearances of God

One theory says His characteristics are His personality. Another says His attributes are displayed in His ultimate powers, shown in the universe, earth, humankind, or nature. Here these two types of characteristics of God are His features, and his powerful traits examined. Although these two of God's many aspects prior need they might not be the strongest or the most important.

God in Man: When we say God in man, the perception is Jesus Christ in man. Jesus Christ came as the Word of God to be a sacrifice. The content of God is not containable within an object; He is too holy. The Holy Spirit is the Spirit of God. He is one of the Trinity. The primary purpose of the Trinity is to be the whole existence of the God of reality. He can perform the entire personages of God but always point to the exact godhead. His job is to transport their work into existence. He is the mover of all existence.

A Testimony

Christianity is a life-changing religious experience. The change causes an unbeliever to become a believer in the unseeable things of God. The meat on the bone is getting to know God through our Lord and Savior, Jesus Christ. There are steps to becoming a child of God, but first, God has to call you, but there are other ways to become a Christian. However, you must have faith that Jesus Christ is the Son of God.

This part of the book discusses the God of Christianity. The testaments classify God as the God of the Old Testament and the New Testament. God is God, no matter what setting we place Him. When I think of God, I see Him as a provider, He knows the sorrows of humanity. My friend died last week, and her daughter calls me to let me know. I believe, God is good all the time. At that moment, I could tell her how God kept me in the time of losing a loved one. I asked God to help me keep praying for her and her family.

I know what belief in the power of God can do. It can change lives and hearts of pain. His Spirit is sweet and will comfort in times of hardship. I know because he settled my bleeding heart on many occasions. This section of the book reinforced my Christian experience because it covers the broad spectrum of Christianity.

CHAPTER VI
WHO IS JESUS

God in the Earth

The Word of God is Jesus Christ, and Jesus Christ is the Word of God. He is the Son of God who offered true Salvation to the entire world. Jesus represented God and man of a divine nature to combat evil." The Salvation that Jesus gives is God's gift to empower humankind to live by God's covenant agreements. Salvation enables people to think and live by God's standards. The gift of Salvation transforms humanity to live a life after the teachings of Jesus Christ.

The gift of Salvation offers to resolve the insufficiency of humanity's needs brought on by Satan. Humanity's deficiency separates them from God that needed to be "eradicated." Jesus demolished Satan's power when he rose from the dead destroying the evil rule over behaviors of humans. Notes: taken from Christian Theology pg. 742

For the possibility of the redeeming feature of Salvation to happen, Jesus had to offer himself as a sacrifice. As a human serving in place of God, Jesus Christ upheld His divine nature." Jesus represents God's perfect picture in human form, for no one could have sacrificed himself or herself except God to redeem humankind. In Christ, all the fullness of the Deity lives in bodily form."

Jesus came in the form of a man and acted in God's capacity, revealing the full revelation of God's picture in the flesh. Jesus possesses the Godlike powers of omnipresence and omniscience, but he chooses not to exercise them while acting in a human's capacity. He had courage but limited use of His capabilities and capacities. He said this is not my fight, but if "I call on my Father" for help, He will send enough war angles to oversee any adverse situation, I find the need to be resolved.

The historical Jesus: The genealogy and Nativity of Jesus reveal differently in each Synoptic Gospels, but John exclusively looks at the life of Jesus as divine revelation. Jesus was born to Mary, the wife of Joseph. Jesus' ancestry traces him through Adam to God. The Synoptic Gospels describe Jesus' birth as a virgin named Mary in Bethlehem in fulfillment of prophecy. The Holy Spirit in Mary's womb miraculously conceived Jesus when she was still a virgin. In John's Gospel, the apostles and John tells of the revelation of Jesus as the beginning of humanity. Notes are taken from John 1:1-5 A2. Cited by John 1: 1-5 [A2]

John reveals the coming of Jesus in revelation: "There was a man sent from God, whose name was John He came as a witness to testify to the light so that all might believe through him. He was not the light, but he came to testify of the light. The true light, which enlightens everyone, was coming onto the world." Cited by John 1:7 [A2].

Jesus, the man, or Jesus the God: In the Synoptics, When Jesus takes bread, breaks it, and gives it to the disciples. He said, "This is my body, which is given for you." He then asked them to drink from the cup. Jesus said, "This cup that is poured out for you is the new covenant in my blood" (Luke 22:19–20). He gave his broken body and his scarce blood as a sacrifice for humanity to obtain Salvation.

In John 18:36, Jesus said, "My kingdom is not from this world," even though He was judged and condemned for claims, such as blasphemy saying He is the Son of God and the savior to the world. Jesus announced that his kingdom was not of this world and told humanity there is another government ruling under a different domain. He said to them that in his Father's house are many mansions; he would go and prepare room for them there.

When Jesus died, an earthquake took place, and a Roman centurion terrified of the events of the earthquake stated that Jesus was the Son of God. The heavy curtain at the Temple splits down the middle to signify the wall of protection was broken down, thus allowing all access to God's throne.

The Mission of Jesus: Jesus's mission started with the creation in the Old Testament. Geneses Chapter One begins with, "In the beginning was the Word and the Word was with God, and God said." The Old Testament gives glimpses of God's Word interacting with humankind; throughout the Old Testament, especially the first five books called the Pentateuch or Torah. The Old Testament shows humankind's relationship with God through Covenants (Word of God). Still, the New Testament people establish a relationship with God through Jesus Christ as the Word of God (New Covenant).

The four authorized gospels, Matthew, Mark, Luke, and John are the principal sources for the life and message of Jesus, but the first three, called the Synoptic Gospels, hold the most sources of information about the life and death of Jesus. On the other hand, the Gospel of John speaks of his life in symbolic terms.

Teachings of Jesus: In the Synoptics, Jesus promises entrance into the Kingdom for those who accept his message (Mark 10:13–27). Jesus talks of the "Son of Man, an apocalyptic figure who would come to gather the chosen. He tells the crowd to repent of their sins and to devote themselves entirely to God. One of Jesus' teachings is the greatest commandment. He said, "You shall love the Lord your God with all your heart, and with all your soul, and with your entire mind. He said the second command is, 'You shall love your neighbor as yourself" (Matthew 22:37–39). Jesus also taught other ethical teachings, including loving your enemies, refraining from hating and lusting, turning the other cheek, and forgiving people who have sinned against them. Cited from Matthew 5–7

John's Gospel presents the teachings of Jesus not as his preaching but as divine revelation. John the Baptist sees Jesus and calls him the Lamb of God. John the Baptist said in John 3:34: "He whom God has sent speaks the Words of God, for he gives the Spirit without measure." Jesus said about his teaching. "My teaching is God's not mine, but Him who sent me." He asserts the same thing in John 14:10: "Do you not believe that I am in the Father and the Father is in me? The words that I say to you I do not speak on my own, but the Father who dwells in Me does His works." Cited from [A2]

Jesus' Teaching and Religious Personality: The thoughts of Jesus were expressed in His teaching as sound doctrine. Sound doctrine produces a change in the appearance of the hearts of humanity. Jesus came into this world to teach humanity words of wisdom to a holy living. For society to accept the terms of Jesus will help them to transform into the image of Christ is the ultimate goal of the Christians' belief and the primary reason Christ came into the world to seek out unbelievers.

Jesus' moral authority resided in the quality of his teaching and His religious personality. Jesus is God incarnated in the flesh and showed forth His power with the use of God's language and the images of God, along with the His divinity. Jesus' ethical ideology established His authority to teach religious teaching. Jesus's teachings about God gave Him the authority to teach God's universal fatherhood and the power to conduct holy dominantly.

The Sermons of Jesus: Most powerful sermons of Jesus are the Sermons on the Mounts. The calming of the storm, the feeding of the 5,000, and walking on water. As a whole theme, the Bible shows the is redemption work of Jesus Christ, the world's Savior. The Bible is a record of God's revelation, which has to do with humankind's Salvation brought with Jesus' sacrifice. God spoke in times past unto the fathers by the prophets, but in these last days spoken unto humanity by his Son. Cited from Hebrews 1:1-2 [A2]

His purpose in the world: McGrath's research on the identity and significance of Jesus Christ disclosed two realities of His authority. First, Jesus' power resided in the quality of His teaching and religious personality. The second affirmed Jesus is God incarnated in the flesh. Notes: Taken from McGrath; pg. 95

The Trinity: The Trinity represents three entities of the Godhead. The three are God the Father, God the Son, and God the Holy Spirit. Throughout the Bible, in the Old Testament and the Old Testament, God's orientation is recognized as one. Even so, there are passages that give accounts of different bodies that represent the title of God. Deuteronomy 6:4 expresses a unity of division as one. The Holy Spirit is recognized as God because he possesses an attribute that only God has, like omniscience. Notes: taken from 1 Cor. 12:20 [A2].

Matthew 28:19 best states both the oneness and Threeness of the unity of the one God. The undivided essence of God belongs equally to each of the three persons of the Trinity. The Godhead represents God as the author of all things, His Son as the Word that created it, and the Spirit is the power to move items into existence.

The Word of God: The Word of God is Jesus Christ. Jesus Christ is the Word of God, or the Son of God offers God's real thoughts to the world. He came from heaven with the message of God to humanity, understanding regarding righteous life living. Jesus Christ brought to society a new way to worship God called Salvation. Salvation is the solution to man's crisis of life living. Redemption offers all things humans need to live righteous lives to please God. The gospel of Christianity provides the message of Salvation, a system of empowerment to defeat powerless living.

Jesus' teachings centered along the line of revelations. In St John's book, John introduces Him as the Lamb of God who takes away the world's sins. This revelation was fulfilled and disclosed in the Old Testament and the New that one man would take away the world's evils. The disclosures of Jesus coming into the world reveal other tasks He would accomplish.

Jesus said the words He spoke were from God. Isiah 8:20 affirms Jesus' statement. "To the Law and the testimony if they speak not according to His word; it is because there is no light in them." Another statement He made; He told the crowd they are the light of the world. If they are the light of the world and lose the taste for truth, their light will not shine for the world to see God.

The entire Bible speaks about the redemptive work of Jesus. His work was to free humanity from the punishment, guilt, and dominion of sin. Jesus is the redeemer God sacrifice to set humanity free from Satan's ownership of their souls. As a human man, Jesus proved He could live a life pleasing to God. In all His ways, He was about performing God's business.

CHAPTER VII
GOD OF THE HOLY SPIRIT

God's Time

God has conversed with people in many ways. In the Old Testament, God connected with people through prophets, but in the New Testament, He linked with people through His Son, Jesus Christ. Jesua said He had to go back to God the Father to send back the Holy Spirit. Although the Holy Spirit of God appeared in the Old Testament in many instances, in the New Testament, Jesus said the Father would send the Spirit to dwell in humankind.

The Spirit of God is the gift Jesus Christ said he would receive of God to send to the apostles on the day of Pentecost. Jesus told them the Holy Spirit would guild them into all truth, He would comfort them, and He would show them how to live holy, righteous lives. The Holy Spirit is the gift of Salvation Jesus said he gives to the world

The Holy Spirit, just like Jesus has always been with God from the beginning of time. In Genesis, the first chapter gives an account of this fact. "In the beginning, the earth was without form and void; and darkness was upon the deep face. And the Spirit of God moved upon the face of the waters." A2 (Genesis 1:2, Scofield)

The Works of the Holy Spirit

The Holy Spirit's role in the Old Testament is much like His role in the New Testament. Just like His work in history is just like His role today and tomorrow. The Holy Spirit works in four general areas: regeneration, indwelling (or filling), restraint, and empowerment for the service of God. Notes: taken from Charles Ryrie; pg. 395-452)

Regeneration: The first area of the Spirit's work is in the process of renewal. Another word for regeneration is "rebirth," from which we get the concept of being "born again." The proof of this foundation is in John's gospel: "I tell you the truth; no one can see the Kingdom of God unless he is born again." What does this have to do with the Holy Spirit's work in the Old Testament? Jesus' dialogue with Nicodemus, He had this to say, "You must be born again. Cited by John 3: 3-10

He said to Nicodemus. He should have known that the Holy Spirit brought the gift of Salvation written in the Old Testament scriptures. For instance, Moses told the Israelites before entering the promised land that "The Lord your God will circumcise your hearts and the hearts of your descendants, so that you may love him with all your heart and with all your soul, and live" (Deuteronomy 30:6). This circumcision of the heart is the work of God's Spirit and accomplished only by Him. Notes: taken from Charles Ryrie; pg. 395-452

The fruit of the Spirit's regenerating work is faith (Ephesians 2:8). In the book, Hebrews in chapter [11] declared the Old Testament scriptures prophecy that many are filled with the Holy Spirit. The supposes the theory that religion produced is by the regenerating power of the Holy Spirit. In that case, this must be the case for Old Testament saints who looked ahead to the cross, believing that what God had promised concerning their redemption would happen. They saw the promises and "welcomed them from a distance" (Hebrews 11:13), accepting by faith that what God had promised, He would also bring to pass. Notes: taken from Charles Ryrie; pg. 395-452

Indwelling: The second aspect of the Spirit's work is the indwelling or filling. Here is where the significant difference between the Spirit's roles in the Old and New Testaments is apparent. The Old Testaments revealed the Spirit did not dwell in believers, but hoovered over them until the work God had them to do was completed. The New Testament teaches the Holy Spirit is permanent indwelling in believers (1 Corinthians 3:16-17; 6:19-20). When believers place their faith in Christ for Salvation, the Holy Spirit comes to live within Saints. The Apostle Paul calls this eternal indwelling the "guarantee of Saint's inheritance" (Ephesians 1:13-14).

In contrast to this work in the New Testament, the Old Testament's indwelling was selective and temporary. The Spirit "came upon" such Old Testament people as Joshua (Numbers 27:18), David (I Samuel 16:12-13), and even Saul (I Samuel 10:10). In the book of Judges, we see the Spirit "coming upon" the various judges God raised to deliver Israel from their oppressors.

The indwelling was a sign of God's favor upon that individual (in the case of David). If the blessings of God's gift left an individual, the Spirit would depart (e.g., in Saul's claim in (I Samuel 16:14). Finally, the Spirit "coming upon" an individual does not always indicate that person's spiritual condition (e.g., Saul, Samson, and many of the judges). Therefore, in the New Testament, the Spirit only indwells in believers, and that indwelling is permanent. The Spirit came upon certain Old Testament individuals for a specific task. When the completion of the job, the Spirit departed from that person. Notes: Taken from Charles Ryrie; pg. 395-452

Restraint of Sin: The third aspect of the Spirit's work in the Old Testament is His restraint of sin. Genesis 6:3 would seem to indicate that the Holy Spirit restrains man's sinfulness, and that restraint is removed when the patience of God regarding sin reaches a "boiling point." This thought echoed in II Thessalonians 2:3-8 when a growing apostasy will signal the coming of God's judgment in the end times, until the preordained time when the "man of lawlessness" (v. 3) is revealed is when the Holy Spirit loses the restrains of the power of Satan. Notes: Taken from Charles Ryrie; pg. 395-452

Imparting Spiritual Gifts: The fourth and final aspect of the Spirit's work in the Old Testament is granting serviceability. Much like the way spiritual gifts operate in the New Testament, Spirit would give specific individual services. Consider the example of Bezalel in Exodus 31:2-5. His gift of art worked in the building of the Tabernacle. He was filled with the Spirit of God with wisdom, understanding. (e.g., Saul and David).

We could also mention the Spirit's role in creation. Genesis 1:2 speaks of the Spirit "hovering over the waters" and supervising the work of creation. Similarly, the Spirit is responsible for the work of the new creation (II Corinthians 5:17) as He is bringing people into the Kingdom of God through regeneration. Notes: Charles Ryrie; pg. 395-452

Overall, the Spirit performs much of the same functions in Old Testament times as He does in this current age. The significant difference is the permanent indwelling of the Spirit in believers now. As Jesus said regarding this change in the Spirit's ministry, "But you know him, for he lives with you and will be in you" (John 14:17). Notes: Charles Ryrie; pg. 395-452

The Authority of the Holy Spirit: The Spirit is the Spirit of God. Therefore, He is God. His appellations showed divinity when He referred to the Spirit of Jesus (I Cor. 6:11) and referred to the Spirit of God. His authority demonstrated is His attributes are the same as God's, for example, omniscience (Isa. 40:13) and omnipotence by His work in Creation (Job. 33:4; Ps. 104:30). He is the Church's helper, guide, and sanctifier. Notes: Charles Ryrie; pg. 397

Characteristics of the Holy Spirit in the believer: Jesus' likeness shows the attributes of Christ. When referring to Christ, His works point to, His companionship to others and the spiritual power while on earth. Paul listed the characteristics of a believer when filled with the Holy Spirit. He said that person would show four evidence of being Spirit-filled: praising and worshipping God, singing, making melody in the heart, and giving thanks.

The gift of Salvation theory reveals man gains a sinless life by faith, other than using his reason. He seeks God through trust to obtain the gift of salvation. This gift never will be forfeited, except if he decides not to fulfill the faith covenant, he made with God. God's gift of Salvation is obtainable through Jesus Christ. The Holy Spirit is the carrier of the gift and manifests in the bodies of believers.

Salvation is a term used worldwide in many faiths. The faith of a Christian reveals God's gift of Salvation that sanctifies believers to become a child of God. In Hinduism, its meaning has changed through time and ended in moderation of Salvation. It means to worship only in a spiritual way, making other ways obsolete. However, Muslims do not accept the term Salvation' in the vocabulary of Islam.

Carrier of the Gift of Salvation: Jesus told His disciples He would leave, but He would send back the Holy Spirit. He said that the Holy

Spirit would lead them into all truth. Truth has been a tremendously controversial word for theologians and philosophers. Socrates, in his analogy of truth, said, "What is truth." The definition of truth is a fact. It is a fact that there is a Holy Spirit, whose existence is not provable only if one does believe in His works. In every discipline, specific rules, guidelines, and procedures are followed, and Christianity is no exception.

CHAPTER VIII
THE MISSION OF
THE CHURCH

The Great Gospel

The Church's mission is to go into the world and preach Christ. There are other commands Christ tells the church to perform, but this was his first command. It is high time that the Church stands on God's side and tells the world thus says the Lord. The Lord says preach repentance.

The Church reveals the Way, the Truth, and the Light: Jesus gave the baton to His disciples, who gave it to the church and the church is to go into the world and make disciples. The authority to teach Salvation is now in the hands of the Church.

Powers at War: The forces of God and Satan's strengths, which are at war and this war, have to do with humanity. Therefore, society must understand the reasons for the mission of the church. Humanity is evaluated by the powers of God of righteousness and evils. They are to distinguish between rights and wrongs. God understands the authority of Satan, and He gave the Church the authority to show society how to defeat him and live righteous lives that are pleasing to God.

The Power of the Word of God: The Church uses "in the name of Jesus" to beat the adversary, Satan. The scriptures tell believers that some will plant a seed, another will water it, and another will cultivate it. The duties of the Church in the field are centered around saving the unbelievers. They are not to expect immediate change but continued the sanctification steps until that person will change to see God's glory.

According to God's plan for the Church, they offered the plan of Salvation, offering them the power to live good and righteous lives to stay within God's grasp. The Name of Jesus is the power for humankind to get rid of evil forces in their lives. Live moral lives according to God's will. Christians believe without God's guidance; society is short in its thinking to rule this world.

Jesus worked hard to begin the Christian Church. His body adores, protects, and allows the church believers to learn to use power in His name to win spiritual warfare. "For they wrestle not against flesh and blood, but principalities, against powers, against the rulers of the darkness of this world, against spiritual wickedness in high places." Cited from Philippians 6:12.

Gift of Salvation: God gave the world a part of Him when He allows His Spirit to dwell in believers. The gift of Salvation is the Holy Spirit working in believers to make a righteous change. The change is a process from sanctification to sanctification.

CHAPTER IX
THE OPPONENT OF GOD

The Ruling Prince of the Air

Christianity gives the name Satan to a former Archangel of God. He held the position of Minister of Music in heaven. Satan, in an arrogant tone, said I could rule in place of God. He recruited an army of angels, and they fought against the army of God. The Archangel Michael, leader of the Army of God, won the battle. He threw Satan and His demons (former angles) out of heaven and landed on earth. The Bible declared, "Woe to you, O earth and sea, for the devil has come down unto you in great wrath because he knows that his time is short." Cited from Revelation 12:12 [A2].

He rules the earth under the title of the Prince of the Air. He possesses and uses powers opposite to God's Words. His influence was resolved by Jesus, the Word of God. The Word of God came to earth as a man; he died and came back from the dead with the keys of heaven and hell. He has the power to rule heaven, earth, and hell. Jesus stopped Satan's rule over humanity's souls, to take their souls to hell to live in total evilness for eternity. Hell is a place God prepared for Satan and His demons to live, but because of humanity's sinful nature, their destiny is hell as well. The life, death, and resurrection of Jesus paid the price to release humanity's minds and souls from under Satan's rule. Now humanity has the power to receive and use the promises of God.

Humanity's thoughts of Good and Evil

The tedious task of humanity is trying to demythologize the good or evil in their minds and lives. Even so, it is their responsibility to separate, choose, and justify the use of God's powers over the powers of

Satan. Throughout the Bible, good and evil forces are seen performing good or evil acts in humanity's lives. Biblical history tells of the wars over the entitlement of the minds and souls of humankind. The thoughts and souls of humanity have extraordinary significance to God and Satan. The picture the Bible shows, God has a great desire to preserve human life and its societies; but Satan's greatest desire is to destroy them. Humanity must understand the reasons behind their choices of words and behaviors.

Humanity created was to live under God's laws, a life-of-hope pleasing to the creator, but they rebelled. Humankind is evaluated continuously under God's powers of good and the opposite powers of God's Word to determine if they are worthy to be called a child of God. In life, they have confessed their belief in the opposite Words of God, which shows their confidence in believing and experiencing depravity in the face of powerless living. Their wrong choice or their desires take them out of the will of God's Plan of Salvation for them.

Humanity can choose to live according to the plan of God. The Salvation plan is God's power in humanity's life to enable them to live a good life and enjoy their laborers' fruits. Under God's power of Salvation, they are empowered with the seal of God's Holy Spirit to live good and righteous lives. The first people forfeited humankind's stay in the Garden of Eden's original economy. Today they can live in the spiritual Kingdom of Heaven, another perfect economy of God. They are empowered with the power of the Spirit of God to resist Satan. They transform their minds to be like Christ if they keep their minds in heavenly places when their minds focus on His Words of life.

Satan and Sin

God's judgment in history happened because of evil influences, which caused God's created order to be compromised. The devil masked his deceptive words to deceive the first woman and man. His remarks are free, desirable, and harmless, but his whole purposes were to get them to sin against God. Satan and his demons are the cosmic powers of evil and disorder. When humanity chooses to live an obedient life to Christ, they experience the ability to honor God and put Him as the ruler of their minds and heart. Then and only then will they have a power greater than Satan does over their lives.

God's promises to humanity are in effect at the beginning of time, and they will stay in effect until the end times. He said, "if you disobey me, you will surely die. (Gen. 3:1-2) Satan still uses the same tactics he used at the beginning of time. He starts with convening humanity to reason with him about their obedience to God, or he gets them to disregard the Words of God. Satan also influences society to question the authority of God. For example, in the Garden of Eden, he told the woman to eat the fruit from the tree of good and evil knowledge, and she will become wise like God knowing good and evil. God lied to you because He does want you to be equal with Him. Go ahead and disobey Him; you will surely not die as God promised.

In addition, the devil still utilizes humanity's curiosity to get them to question the commands of God. His three tactics are first; he used temptation to satisfy the hunger they think needs immediate gratification. Next, Satan uses the allure of worship of idols to make humans believe they are more important than worshiping God. Then he also uses the opposite of the Words of God to contradict God's Words.

FINAL REMARKS

Destines after Death: People believe there are three ways to live after death. Some say their exit ticket after life is to go to heaven, while others say hell is real; still, others say they live in heaven and hell now on earth, and others do not believe in either. The perception of life after death is a concept in humanity's minds, and it cannot be determined only if they chose to accept where they are destined to go. Going to heaven or hell are promises of God. All of God's promises are true.

REFERENCE OF GOD
OF THE HOLY BIBLE

1. August Strong Systematic theology(1-Eiselen, Lewis, Downey, pg. 11) or Strong, Augustus Hopkins, 1836-1921. Systematic Theology: a Compendium Designed for the Use of Theological Students. Valley Forge, Pa.: The Judson Press, 1907.
2. Scobie, Charles H.H. The Ways of Our God, Grand Rapids, Michigan: William B. Eerdmans Publishing Company, 2003, pg. 108) http://web.mnstate.edu/gracyk/courses/web%20 publishing/aquinasFiveWays).
3. Erickson, Millard J. Christian Theology, Grand Rapids, Michigan: Baker Books, 1999, pgs. 901-919
4. https://www.usgs.gov/special-topic/water-science-school/science/water-you-water-and-human-body?qt-science_center_objects=0#qt-science_center_objects
5. McGrath, Alister E. Christian Theology, Malden, Massachusetts, 2001
6. Esposito, John L, Fasching Darrell J., and Lewis Todd. World of Religions Today, Oxford, NY: Oxford University Press, 2009
7. Clevenot, Michel. Materialist Approaches to the Bible, Maryknoll, NY: Orbis Books, 1985
8. https://www.eastern.edu/about/vision-mission-faith/wxg

"the GOD OF THE HOLY BIBLE ends."

PART II

RELIGIONS AND PHILOSOPHIES

CHAPTER I
KNOWN FACTS
ABOUT RELIGION

Culture mirrors religion, and religion reflects culture. Even so, there must be a precise definition that defines the concept of religion. For example, India has a Caste economic system related to its faith to its deities; based on higher authority levels. The Caste economy classified people as like worship. The basis of religious belief is on the higher levels of gods. Only certain people can worship certain gods, as certain people can become educated or work in government jobs. Some say the culture and religions enhance each other to gain stability within the country, but critics differ in their opinions.

Definition of Religion

Religion is "a set of beliefs." [A1] The concept of faith has to do with worshiping God (s) and establishing a moral system. The universality of religions is about the erection of temples, pyramids, or other monuments that the society raised as the expression of faith in the deity (s). The definition defines the similarities of religions' basis but does not represent beliefs that express themselves (culture). Religions are a way to worship God (s) and follow a moral code.

The Great Transition

The tribal godlike transition went from worshiping the sun, moon, stars, man, and animals to spiritualism and, from there, to religion. In ancient times, tribal life consisted of Indigenous groups of humans who lived close to nature's rhythms but lived only among their tribes. These people created myths to live by giving people hope in times of natural distress. In time passed, the concept of God played a significant factor in their lives. When a leader or high-ranking leader of a group said they have been in contact with God and can use His powers, then most clans would believe and follow that leader's teachings without controversy.

As time moved forward, the Indigenous groups of humans merged to live in cities. Their lifestyles were governed by a single way of living, still manipulated by others many spiritual beliefs, customs, and thoughts that they made up about stories of God. Stories told were among them about powers of nature that govern human destiny, which portrayed was as "food production," "natural phenomena," "animals," "spirits," and were regard as "ancestors." [1]

CHAPTER II
INDIGENOUS RELIGIONS

Cultures had many ancient belief systems that existed and moved with them from tribal lifestyles and traveled throughout history to establish a social group of religions, languages, and governments. Throughout history, they contended to understand God's vision and holy things. Finally, they emerged to define the right expressions of the great thoughts about the one God of good and mercy with great intentions for all humanity.

Religion has always been a part of people's baseline of learning. The first religious system of humanity started with "theology, the biblical theory about God." [A2] Cultures throughout the world began with religious teaching for life guidance. Most believe that ethics, law, and social responsibility materialize from the religious thought of righteous living. The classification of religious belief among superstition has given man his perceptions of right and wrong.

Another teaching that influenced humanity's thought came later, science, a modern systematic way of thinking based on evidence and logic. The contemporary belief of man believes all things need to be proven, especially those he cannot see. Believing in things not seen is unthinkable to science. They refuse to accept things taught by religion. They say unseen things cannot happen because they cannot see them. The spiritual events, even though the concept of spirituality is the same as man's thought process, which is unseen until it materializes on earth. There is no difference between the things seen and unseen in human minds because both are concepts. deemed reality.

Spiritualism to Religions

Creating thoughts of relationships with the unknown powers of nature to establish protection was all tribal life knew to believe that tribal life could be a more comfortable place to live. These strange powers of nature advanced the meaning of natural phenomena beyond the understanding of tribal beliefs but finally became manageable. In cities, Tribal leaders became rulers, such as kings and pharaohs who claimed they had powers to rule nature.

These rulers had to lead and protect their city dwellers, and the best way to win the hearts of many is to have God on their sides to win battles or say they were God themselves. When a tribal leader pronounced the images of winning wars, seeing fertility among the women, bearing childbirths, and increasing military power, wealth and economic stability flourished because they said God was on their side. When a city declared God was on its size, other cultures would stand down, fear them, and show respect.

Expressions of Religions

Religion is a universal phenomenon in most cultures, a type of faith practice recognizing a supreme power greater than humanity. Religion exists in every society, from the most primitive to the most culturally advanced. Religion is not only universal; it is also one of the features separating man from the animal world. Faith in religion is the picture of humankind's path to reach God.

Today, there are many types of religious systems. Many have come, and many have gone. Over the years, four types of religions have sprung up and remained significant in the cultures of the world. First, indigenous faith not categorized among the world's major religions is on the continents of Africa and America. The many types of religions within an Indigenous faith are the traditional way of spiritual worship. The second religious base originated in the East. India, China, and Japanese religions are different but have some similarities. The third origination of religion happens in the Middle East. The beliefs of these religions isolated were in lands far away from each other. Today, they have reached each other's land fronts, and their language of faiths taught in lands that they did not originate from throughout the world.

There is no preservation of native religions written for understanding these religions is not known, and their practices are unclear.

In most cases, these religions are in America and Africa; and are designated in many different clans but the same race of people. The Native Americans and individual Africans have common characteristics, and religious practices still reveal an "animistic view of nature." [1]

Religions of Africa and North America: All religions still have indigenous nature according to scientific theory. Modernization has advanced knowledge about religion. Instead of a primitive way of believing, science has engaged their thoughts to accept modern technology ways. The transformation of praying to unknown gods helped them with fertility, childbirth, and survival to believe in science. Science provides models to preserve Indigenous people's lives and culture worldwide without acknowledging God.

The purpose of religion is to allow people to experience spiritualism, have faith, and believe in supernatural beliefs that emphasize the spiritual nature of existence and the afterlife. However, it would be nice to adapt to each other's culture of religions. Secularism started this concept, but they left out God, a vital part of humanity's cultures, and their faith of beliefs in God. The introduction of "cultural innovation" [1] to engage others to adapt to other religions' beliefs and practices is vital in advancing religion. This is the new way of the future of theology.

CHAPTER III
THE EASTERN RELIGIONS
& PHILOSOPHIES

The philosophies or religions of the East are India, China, Japan, and Korea. Two of the world's major spiritual faiths are India (Hinduism) and China (Buddhism). Japan teaches Confucianism and Taoism. In Korea, Confucianism establishes as the state philosophy, but Buddhism and Christianity have gained South Korean roots. Still, since North and South Korea's division into two countries, religion in South Korea is acceptable. Still, the majority of South Koreans have no religious affiliation or follow folk religions. The belief in North Korea is by state atheism, in which freedom of religion is nonexistent. Experts regard the Juche ideology, which promotes the North Korean cult of personality, as a national religion. Judaism, Islam, and Christianity religions are called Abrahamic religions of the Middle East.

Common affiliations: The chain that links the philosophies or religions is the terminologies. There are four basic terms used throughout Hinduism and Buddhism. Each has to do with a way of life and the pathways to life or God.

Basic Vocabulary: The Buddha presents the "three bits of knowledge" (avijja) – a term used in the Vedic tradition to describe knowledge of the Vedas – as being "not texts, but things that he had experienced." The actual "three bits of knowledge" constitute the process of achieving enlightenment, which the Buddha attained in the three watches of his enlightenment night.

Karma: Karma is a term used in both philosophies of Buddhism and Hinduism. It denotes "the entire cycle of cause and effect as described in the doctrines of cosmologies. The word means to act or activity (also called karma-phala, "the fruits of action). Karma is a central part of Buddhist teachings. In Buddha's teaching, karma is a direct, intentional act of good or evil that shows the result of a person's word, thought, or action in life. In Buddhism, the basis for good and bad karma is sila (moral conduct), which goes hand in hand with meditation and wisdom.

Dharma: The four significant philosophies on the continent of Asia are Hinduism, Buddhism, Jainism (Jaina Dharma), and Sikhism (Sikha Dharma). Dharma can refer to religious duty and mean social order, right conduct, or virtue. Dharma means Natural Law, Reality, or Duty. Its significance for spirituality and religion is considered the Way of the Higher Truths. The general concept of dharma forms a basis for philosophies, beliefs, and practices originating in India. They retain the centrality of dharma in their teachings. According to the tradition, Dharma Yukam, Moksha, or Nirvana (personal liberation) in these traditions, beings that live in harmony with dharma proceed more quickly.

Buddha: The term "Buddha" appeared in Hindu scriptures before the birth of Gautama Buddha. In the Vayu Parana, sage Daksha calls Lord Shiva Buddha. One of Hinduism's principal deities in Shaivism is Shiva, also known as Mahadeva, the Great God, considered the Supreme Being.

Faiths of India: The country of India's supreme law is the Constitution (IAST: Bhāratīya Saṃvidhāna). The document is the "framework of government institutions' political code, structure, procedures, powers, and duties." [2] It sets out the fundamental rights, directive principles, and responsibilities" [2] of its citizens. India's constitution (original 1950) declares India a sovereign, socialist, secular, democratic republic. It assures its citizens of justice, equality, and liberty. It endeavors to promote society.

The major languages spoken in India belong to several language families. The major ones are the Indo-Aryan languages spoken by 78.05% of Indians and the Dravidian languages spoken by 19.64% of Indians. [2] Hinduism and Buddhism share philosophies in the Ganges culture of northern India and certain parts of the continent of Asia. The belief system is common, but the difference in cultures.

The Caste system in India is under the rulers and large assemblies of military monks. The East India Company officials adopted constitutional laws segregated by religion and Caste. The fundamental rights in India are the spiritual development of citizens of India. As these rights are implied or essential for the existence and all-round development of individuals

India is the subcontinent that gave birth to four major religions in the world. Namely, Hinduism, Buddhism, Jainism, and Sikhism—collectively known as Dharma religions that believe Moksha is the supreme state of the Atman. The religious characteristics of India are a diversity of religious beliefs and practices. The preamble of the Indian constitution states that India is a secular state.

India's various religions are in Japan, China, Korea, Vietnam, Burma, Cambodia, and Thailand. The religions believe in many gods but claim one Sikhism is the exception. (Sikhism, One God from the religion of Islam) Reincarnation is one of the major themes of these religions. These religions' ultimate concern is that people can relax from the "cycle of life, death, and rebirth." [3] The goal appeals to the aid of the gods. Others' actions, or lack thereof, are to work out their problems.

Hinduism is the central practice of religion in the northern territory of India. Along with the traditions of Hinduism are Islam, Sikhism, Christianity, and Jainism. Most Hindus in India belong to Shaivite and Vaishnavite denominations. Hindus (Hindustani) are an ethical group of people who use Hinduism to identify themselves geographically, culturally, ethnically, or religiously. The Hindu population in India is 80 percent. Notes: Taken from Brotammoca/India history.com/1/21

Hinduism comprises several and various systems of beliefs, philosophy, and rituals. Although the name Hinduism is new, the British devised it in the first decades of the 19th century. [3] However, in the Indus valley, civilization (BCE third–2nd millennium) was the earliest hint of Hinduism tradition. As some scholars hold, Hinduism is the oldest living religion on earth. Its many sacred texts in Sanskrit and vernacular languages served as vehicles for spreading faith to other parts of the world.

In the early 21st century, Hinduism had one billion adherents worldwide and the religion of about 80 percent of India's population. Despite its global presence, Hinduism is best understood through its many distinctive regional manifestations. Hinduism began by asking what people want to follow. In the process of life, Hinduism offers perfection, is inclusive, universal, and genuinely humanistic. Hindus hold people wish for four things: pleasure, success, duty, to be recognized, that brings happiness is marked as perfect.

Hinduism gives four reasons why world success does not satisfy hunger within. First, to have material success, one must get wealth, fame, and power exclusively; one must diminish one's portion. Next, they say, "to drive for success; one seeks an unquenchable thirst." [4] Third, they believe in gaining hedonism; one finite self proves to be too small for enduring interest. Finally, world success cannot satisfy the temporal man; its rewards are temporary.

Hinduism has four paths to the liberation of the soul: First, "the Path of Desire," [4] which Hindus believe locates pleasure and success. The way of desire takes a natural course in life. A dictated desire will fulfill a life's sequence. These desires should not be condemned but fulfilled. There is nothing wrong with fulfilling a passion, but the wrong happens when sad for a desire has become fixated. It was not satisfying.

Next, "the Path of Renunciation." [4] Hinduism identified the path with desire or absence of self-will and self-centeredness. Hinduism distinguishes chronological and psychological age. For example, the same age but different in their maturity Hindus extend this distinction to cover multiple life spans. The consequences of the desire seeker will die with the sense of having had a good life, while the others will be just as good at the same game but find its glories worthless of people's desires.

Going from self-centeredness into the Path of Renunciation, "Hinduism has planted two markers that constitute the Path of Renunciation. [4] The first reads community. In supporting one's own life and others' lives, the importance eliminates individual life of command. The transfer of allegiance gives priority to its claims over one's own life. This transfer marks the first significant step in religion. It produces the faith of duty – after pleasure and success, and gives way to the third step, the great aim of life.

Thus, underlying human self and animating it is a reservoir of being that never dies, is never exhausted, and unrestricted in consciousness and bliss. An infinite center of every life, this "hidden self or Atman," [4] is no less than "Brahman," [4] "Atman-Brahman – a human self," [4] not accounted for until all three entered. The human project is to clean oneself to allow the light to radiate in full display.

Hinduism holds that life aims to transcend imperfections completely by reducing them to three: ones that limit the joy, knowledge, and being that humanity wants. The structures of happiness fall into three subgroups: physical pain, thwarted desires, and boredom, in which emptiness breeds apathy and depression. To all that overcome it is a sense of life's vanity. Note: taken from Huston; pg. 24.

As for the "restricted being," [4] life is third limitation examined humanity to see how a person defines self. The size of their spirits and the range of reality that engages them compared to human beings carry this notion to its logical limit. It posits a self that threads successive lives in how a single life weaves its next moments, the Hindu estimate of human nature's primary point. Humankind is "like kings who, falling victim to amnesia, wander their kingdoms in tatters, not knowing who they are." [4]

Four Paths to God: The way to bring the light of supreme strength, the fullness of wisdom, and unquenchable joy, happens when drawn from it is unceasing. Hinduism discovered that human potential accomplished is through "physical exercises called yoga." [4] Its ultimate goal is union with God. The paths are four diverse ways, identifying the principal types and delineating the programs suited to each. The result is recognition, permeating the entire religion, that there are multiple paths to God, each calling for its distinctive tactic.

The Path to God through Knowledge: This knowledge (Jnana yoga) is an "intuitive discernment that transforms the knower into the likeness of what it knows." [4] It cultivates these proceeds through three stages: the first of which is hearing; through listening to advisers and scriptures. The aspirant introduced the prospect that "one's essential being is being itself." [4] The next step is thinking. Moreover, the fourth step consists of shifting self-identification to one abiding part. This exercise does two things. It drives a wedge between one's self-identification and one's surface self and at the same time forces this self-identification to a deeper level until at last – through a knowledge that is identical to being – one becomes in full what one always was at heart.

The second path to God is love: Love is the most vital path to follow. The way is called "bhakti-yoga," [4] and love is the yoga of love and devotion. It is to direct toward God the love that lies at the base of every heart. To Bhakta, for whom feelings are more important than thoughts, God appears different on each of these counts. First, as healthy love is out-going, the Bhakta will reject all suggestions that the God one loves is oneself, even one's deepest self, and insist on God's otherness. Second, the Bhakta will strive not to identify with God but to adore God with every element of his or her being.

The third path to God through Work: Karma yoga is the way through work. Humanity needs to learn how to work in ways that carry them toward God, not away from God. The spiritual dynamics of work operate in two cases. Hindu doctrine says every act directed toward the external world reacts to the doer. All humanity does for their benefit adds another layer to their ego, and in this thickening, it splits them further from God.

Every act done without thought for themselves diminishes their self-centeredness; until nothing separates from the divine, keeping with this emotionally inclined principle, the person should work for God's sake instead of his or her own. Acts undertook for his or her rewards deemed attached to the service of God. No longer performed as service to God; they are regarded as prompted by God's will and powered by God's energy, which courses through the devotee. ("Thou art the doer, I am the instrument"). [4]

They do this by working in the spirit of detachment: They draw a line between their finite selves and the Infinite Self that underlies them and systematically identify with the former. In terms of work, this means cultivating an active disinterest in "what's in it for me,"[4] whether the reward is cash or recognition. Those rewards are pleasant, but the karma yogi knows their price. If they invested in their inflated self-ego, in doing so, they would thicken the insulation between their current and their true self, and that increases their isolation.

The alternative work is performed detachedly, in virtual dissociation from the empirical self. Identifying with the Eternal, the worker continues to work, but as the practical self performs the deeds, the true self has nothing to do with them. "He, who performs actions without attachment, resigning them to God, is untainted by their effects as the lotus leaf by the water – Bhagavad-Gita." [4]

Psychophysical exercise is the path to God: Raja is a yoga known in India as "the royal (raj) road to reintegration." [4] Designed for persons to require hypotheses intended to confirm or disprove. The assumption that underlies raja yoga is the Hindu doctrine of the human self, which is restated as follows: the self has four layers: bodies, a conscious layer of humanity's mind and the individual subconscious that consists of deposits from their respective histories. Lastly is the conscious mind. The conscious mind is the personal subconscious being itself – infinite, un-thawed, eternal.

Hinduism's fundamental thought is one with Atman attached to certain circles to identify with Brahman. The universal self-identities itself with the eternal core of its personality Atman (Sanskrit: "self," "breath"). [4] The universal self-identity with the eternal essence of the character, after death, either transmigrates to a new life or attains release (moksha) from the bonds of existence. Atman makes the faculties function underlies all the person's activities, as Brahman (the Absolute) underlies the universe's workings. Atman is part of the universal Brahman.

Raja yoga is the estimator of the human self. It leads the inquirer to personal experience beyond and within." [4] The method is introversion. Which intends to drive "the self's psychic energy" [4 to] its deepest part, with raja yoga's hypothesis. However, before humankind can reach the eight steps of its experiment, an attempt to verify must occur.

The ultimate step is the hypothesis.

Now the raja yoga hypothesis introduced an introduction to the eight steps of its premises. The first two steps concern the moral preliminaries common to all four yoga:

Step one: the practice of five abstentions (from injury, lying, stealing, sensuality, and greed)

Step two: the five observances (cleanliness, contentment, self-control, studiousness, and contemplation of the divine).

Step three: the position of the body not to distract the mind ("lotus position")

Step four: the breathing- repose the body to approach a state of suspended animation, and the reason seems disembodies.

Step five: unplug one's sense receptors-to turn concentration from a chance occurrence into a controlled skill and raise the gift to hear nothing.

Step six: the yogi is alone with the mind – works for the power of concentration for the reason psychotic minds.

Step seven: the absentee of entire self-awareness – concentrate progressively deepens.

Step eight: the climactic stage – known as Samadhi – objects vanish by excluding them as poperies of things they are not. Taken from Huston, pg. 41

The stages of life: Hinduism says people are different. People are distinct individuals, but they move through various life stages that call for their schedules. Sets of identities of the first stage prepare to enter the next step and finally to retirement. During the retirement stage, "one becomes inner-directed to the point where it does not matter where one lives. Having discovered the release from limitations synonymous with anonymity, the sannyasin (as those in this final stage) can perceive his real from his finite self wherever he happens to be." [4]

The stations of life: The cardinal Hindu tenet outlook says that people should take different paths toward God and other agendas that are appropriate at various stages of life. The social order of Hinduism is called caste. The outlook for people under this system gives way to the idea that people can best contribute to society, as well as best develop their potential when people fall into one of four groups:

1. Brahmins or seers reflect and show keen intuition to grasp what matters in human life. They are civilization's intellectual and spiritual leaders, such as philosophers, artists, religious leaders, and teachers. Things of the mind and spirit are their raw materials.
2. This group is born to be administrators or organizers, with a genius for orchestrating people and projects in ways that maximize available talents.
3. Vocation as producers is those of artisans and farmers and those of this time as engineers who are skillful in creating the material things on which life depends.
4. Followers are those hired hands, unskilled laborers, and current factory workers.

Notes: taken from Huston, pg. 43

Inequality of pay: The assumption about pay for each group discloses compensation equally rewarded for their service, but this does not mean that they should receive the same pay rate. That would assume that pay is the reward everyone values most. That is not the case. People paid in different coins. Neither wealth nor power interests Brahmins. So "most wrongly cast into the fire, for rewards for their souls would receive respect from the castes that believe in the former ways of doing things." [4]

There is considerable equality, opportunity, and social insurance within each caste. Even so, the castes themselves ranked hierarchically." [4] It shows an underlying egalitarianism. The assumption is that all jivas (individual souls) would move through all four castes in their manifold incarnations, beginning with the lowest.

In this egalitarianism, justice is considered a state in which privileges are proportionate to responsibilities. The upper three castes considered are religiously initiated. They are honored, affluent, and influential, but their obligations are more outstanding. As far as "caste, today means rigidity, exclusiveness, and undeserved privilege." Hindus are working to clear corruption from their policy. [5]

Thou before whom all word is recoil: Hindus insist one must learn what to leave out before speaking to God. Because thoughts and things are finite and God is infinite, the only accurate description of the unsearchable is not this. If a person traverses the length and breadth of the universe, saying of everything you see/conceive, "not this ... not this," what remains will be God. [5]

God is Brahman: The Sanskrit name for God is Brahman, a dual etymology deriving from breathing to be great. The chief attributes are linked with the term Sashi and Ananda. They mean God is being, aware and blessing her reality, utter consciousness, and utterly beyond all possibility of frustration and futility. The basic Hindu view of God if humankind keeps in mind that their understanding of these "attributes only approximate the way they integrated." [5]

Odysseys of the human soul: Individual souls, or jivas, enter the world mysteriously, by God's power. The how and for what reason are unable to comprehend fully. Humans begin as the soul of the simplest form of life but do not vanish with the original bodies' experience of death. In Hinduism, the process by which an individual "jiva passes through a sequence of bodies known as reincarnation or transmigration." [5]

The passage proceeds automatically on the subhuman level. The soul is on an escalator and ascends through increasingly complex animal forms until the human body attains, and things change dramatically within this attainment. For the first time, the jiva knows itself, and with its reflexive awareness comes freedom with responsibility. The mechanism that ties these new acquisitions together is "karma" (the moral law of cause and effect). [5]

The present condition of each interior life, based on how happy it is, how confused or serene, and how much it sees – is an exact product of what it has wanted and done in the past. Equally, one's present thoughts and decisions determine one's future experiences; each act directed upon world reacts to oneself, delivering a chisel blow that sculpts one's destiny. "This notion of a completely moral universe commits Hindu to complete the personal duty." [5]

Karma decrees that every decision must have its inexorable consequences. A jiva that has reached the human level wants nothing more than to taste vast sensory delights. It is a piece of new physical equipment affords. Jiva turns to social conquests as long as wealth, fame, and power remain exciting. When the novelty wears off, they are satisfied, the winner looks for something new and more deeply satisfying to look to duty.

Duty is the total dedication of one's life to one's community. The need for a while, but in time, one discovers that it is going in circles. After the social dedication, the only good that can satisfy the want is the Infinite and Eternal: "Moksha, unconditional release, the general direction is upward." [5] Never during its pilgrimage is the human spirit alone. From start to finish, its nucleus is the "Atman, the God within that seeks release." Instead, in bhakti's understanding, God is one's constant companion, the Friend who understands.

When the individual reaches the goal, the individual soul passes into complete identification with God and loses every trace of its former separateness. Others, wishing to taste sugar, hope that some slight differentiation between the soul and God will remain – a thin line that retains the two-ness required for love and the blissful vision.

An Indian fable capsules this process of coming of age in the universe. The story's point is that the universe is one gigantic Wishing Tree, with branches reaching every heart. The cosmic process decreed some time or other, in this life or another, wishes will be granted – together, of course, with consequences.

Cosmology to moral: Within the Hindu world, there are innumerable galaxies comparable to the earth, each entering an earth form that people precede their ways to God. Ringing each globe meant any more acceptable worlds above and coarser ones below, to which souls repair between incarnations according to their just desserts. Periodically, the thread withdrawn is "the cosmos collapses into a Night of Brahma, and all phenomenal returned to a state of pure potentiality." [5] Even so, the world is mediocre in two senses. The position between better worlds (heavens) above and worse worlds (hells) below is the dilemma. The woven is good and evil, pleasure and pain, knowledge, and ignorance about equal proportions.

Hindus characterize the world as Maya. The world seen is the way humans see it, but that is not the real picture. Non-dual Hinduism is saying that there is something tricky about the world. The trick lies in how the world's materiality and multiplicity pass themselves off as being independently real. "The reality is undifferentiated Brahman throughout, is to say, a rope lying in the dust remains a rope while being mistaken for a snake." [5] Maya is also seductive in the allure with which it adorns the world, trapping humankind for a long time within it and postponing their wish to journey.

The only answer given is that the game is its reward, so too, in some mysterious way, one must be with the world as if a child playing alone, God is the cosmic dancer whose routine is all creatures and all worlds. The cosmos flows in an endless, graceful reenactment from the tireless stream of divine energy. Like the goddess Kali dancing on a prone body while holding a sword and severed head in her hands. Who has heard that more "Hindu temples are dedicated to Shiva (God in his aspect of destroyer whose haunt is the crematorium) than to God as creator and preserver combined?" [5] Those who know these things will not jump quickly to conclude that the Hindu worldview is gentle.

 BUDDHISM

"Buddhism" is a religion and philosophy settled from the teachings of the Buddha (Sanskrit: Awakened One), a teacher who lived in northern India between the mid-sixth and mid-4th centuries BCE (Before the Common Era). Spreading from India to Central and Southeast Asia, China, Korea, and Japan, Buddhism has played a significant role in Asia's spiritual, cultural, and social life. In the 20th century, it spread to the West. Ancient Buddhist scripture and doctrine developed in several closely related literary languages of ancient India, especially Pali and Sanskrit. [A4]

The story of awakening: "A man answered, I am awake; not I am a God. The answer became the tile for what Buddha means." [6]

The Sanskrit root Buddha means to awake and to know. Buddhism is about Gautama's experienced discontent and their search out why. He saw an old man – gaunt, broken-toothed, and trembling as he leaned on his staff on a four-day journey. The next day he saw a body racked with disease, lying by the road. On the thirdly encountered a corpse to discover facts about the aging condition, and death in which he saw a monk with a shaven head, ocher robe, and bowl; and learned from him of a path that renounces the world, but this is not what caused Buddha to go on a quest for enlightenment.

While living in the forest, he searched and moved through three phases. First, he searched out two of the foremost Hindu experts of the day and learned what he could about their traditions. Second, he joined a band of ascetics and gave their way. The experience taught Gautama the futility of asceticism and inspired what was to become his first constructive beam. He learned the principle of "The Middle Way" [6] between the extremes of asceticism and indulgence. The final quest opened to a combination of rigorous thought and mystic concentration along Hinduism's raja yoga lines.

Gautama sat down under a tree known as the Bo Tree (short for Bodhi or enlightenment), vowing not to rise until he had gained his goal. Mara, the Evil One, first paraded him with voluptuous women. Mara failed in her pursuit. Next, Mara challenged Gautama's right to do what he was doing, but Gautama touched the ground to bear witness, and Mara Gautama's mediation deepened until it was the brightness of the true being. "The Great Awakening had arrived. Gautama had gone and replaced by the Buddha." [6]

Mara was waiting to go with one last temptation. How could the Buddha expect people to understand the truth as profound as that which he had discovered? Buddha answered, "There will be some who will understand," and Mara was vanquished forever. Half a century followed in which Buddha accomplished his mission. Notes: taken from Huston, pg. 63

Buddha's daily routine of training monks and overseeing his Order's affairs maintained an unending schedule of public preaching and private counseling. What saved him from burning out under these pressures was s pattern of withdrawal and return. Around the year 483 B.C., Buddha died. A keen sense of mission powered the Buddha's entire life immediately after his enlightenment. He saw in his mind's eye the whole of humanity – milling and lost. His acceptance of his mission without regard for personal cost won India's heart as well as her mind. Notes: taken from Huston, pg. 64

Buddha said to the man who said I am awake. I am God whose faith moved to religion. Buddhism trained in Hinduism it was a reaction to Hindu perversions. Six features of religion appear so regularly to suggest that their seeds are in the human makeup: Authority; ritual; explanation; tradition; parts of grace; and sixth, humankind cannot fathom the Infinite.

The first authority is consultation and advice. The second religion is rituals strengthen humans' bonds and relieve their isolation, making them more than the sum of their parts. Third, faith is an explanation. It calls for answers and theories that soon enter the religious domain. The fourth religion is tradition. It compasses what past generations have learned and bequeathed to the present. Fifth, religion features of grace – the belief and assurance that reality is on humanity's side and can turn on. Finally, religion's traffic is a mystery being finite; the human mind cannot fathom the Infinite that envelops it.

Enlightenment: Truth a spring anew for Buddha. He saw it considering culture. Buddha preached a religion devoid of authority. He worked to break the Brahmin's monopoly on religion and called for individuals to take responsibility for their lives. Buddha preached a faith that skirted speculation. He preached a realign devoid of tradition. He said, "Do not follow hearsays, information handed down, or by the authority of your traditional teachings. When you know of yourselves, These things are good or not so. "Only you then accept or reject them." Notes: taken from Huston, pg. 68

Buddha's perception of religion continues with relation to religion is devoted to tradition; it is intense self-effort and faith barren of the supernatural. He condemned all forms of divination, soothsaying, and forecasting as low arts. He concluded from his own experience that the human mind was capable of powers now referred to as paranormal powers. After Buddha's death, all thoughts of low arts became part of Buddhism. Consequently, original Buddhism presents a version of religion that is unique and, therefore, instructive. Buddhism is scientific; it is pragmatic. Buddhism is therapeutic, psychological, egalitarian, and directed to an individual's inward heart. The words of Buddha "Betake yourselves to no external refuge." Work out your salvation with diligence." Notes: taken from Huston, pgs. 62-69

The Four Noble Truths

The First Noble Truth life is dukkha; that is why life is an experience of suffering. Buddha was that suffering could be relieved. How much life is enjoyable, and at what level is it superficial? Beneath the neon dazzle is darkness; at the core – not of all life but unregenerate life- is the quiet desperation. The Second Noble Truth is the cause of dukkha. He is tanha. Dukkha tanha desires personal fulfillment, but it brings suffering and dignity at others' cost. These demands bring suffering because life's law calls for seeing others as extensions of ourselves, not our rivals.

The third Noble Truth follows logically from the second. If the cause of life dislocation is selfish craving, its cure lies in overcoming Tanah, such passion. If humankind released the narrow limits of self-interest into the vast expanse of universal life, they would be relieved of their torment. The Fourth Noble Truth prescribes how a cure is accomplished. The overcoming of tanha, the way out of humankind's captivity, is through the Eightfold Path.

The Eightfold Path: The eightfold path is the prescription for accomplishing the removal of life's problem tanha the causation). The course consists of eight steps that are prefaced by a preliminary step not explicitly stated, but the Buddha mentions it so often elsewhere that it can be assumed that here he presupposed it. This initial step is the right association.

The (1) first path of right knowledge is the step that calls or/ and provides those truths and the way that leads to locking together. The (2) second path is the right of aspiration to help understand what life's problem is and counsel or offer a change in liberation. This path is true enlightenment. The (3) third path tells of the right of speech to notice it and to allow it to reveal the character inside. The fourth paths give rites to the right behavior of humanity. They are not to kill, not to steal, not to lie, and be unchaste. Notes from Huston, pg. 74

The next four paths are the right of livelihood; Buddha considered spiritual progress impossible if the bunk on one's doings pulls against it. The right effort shows moral exertion. The right mindfulness: Buddha matched with great thinkers who said matched ignorance not with sin but as life's prime adversary. Lastly, the correct absorption answers are found in Hinduja leading to psychophysical exercises. Note: taken from Huston, pgs. 34 &75)

The Concept of Basic Buddhism: The basic concept of Buddhism is nirvana. Buddhists used the name nirvana to reach life goals. Negatively nirvana is the state in which the maggoty of private desire consumed is, and everything that restricts eternal life is exhausted. Affirmatively, it is that eternal life itself. Note: taken from Huston, pg. 77

Is nirvana God? Used accordingly to theologians the word means sometimes call the Godhead. The characteristics of nirvana are permanent. They are stable, imperishable immovable ageless, deathless unborn, and unbecoming. It is power, bliss, and happiness, the secret refuge, the shelter, and the place of unassailable safety; it is the Truth and the supreme Reality. It is good. The goal and the only consummation of humankind is eternal hidden and incomprehensible peace. Note: taken from Huston, pg. 77

The Human Self: Buddha said that humanity does not have a soul. This thought is associated with religion. The "anatta" (no soul) doctrine sounds as odd as his denial of a personal God, but the word the Buddha used carefully examined again. What was the Atta (Pali for the Sanskrit atman or soul) with the Buddha denied? At the time, it had come to signify (a) spiritual substance that, in keeping with the dualistic position of Hinduism, (b) retains its separate identity forever. Buddha rejected both these beliefs. Note: from Huston, pg. 77

His alternative view of selfhood is through his thoughts on transmigration. He did not doubt that reincarnation was a fact, but he disagreed with the way his "Brahmanic" contemporaries conceived of it. He envisions it as some psychic "Pettet" that migrated from body to body. The image of a wave captures his alternative view. Nothing in my next incarnation will be identical to what is in me now, but I will still be "me "in how the wave retained its identity while moving through its successive stages. Notes from Huston, pg. 77

What continues from life to life and unites them is a trajectory, a four-dimensional form, a causal chain of karmic propensities. Casual connection is solidly affirmed; no entity – no physical or psychic substantial substrate – passes from life to life. This denial of a significant soul was only an aspect of Buddha's more complete repudiation of substances of every sort. Notes: taken from Huston, pg. 78

China & Japan's Faiths: Japan is in line with three of the largest national economies globally in terms of nominal GDP and the national economy purchasing power parity. Japan's religious population subscribes to Shinto as its Indigenous religion ranging from about 84 to 96 percent. Many Japanese people practice both Shinto and Buddhism. They can either identify with both religions or describe themselves as non-religious or spiritual. Other religions practiced in Japan are Muslims, Hinduism, Judaism, and Bahá'í Faith the animist beliefs. Notes: taken from https://en.wikibooks.org/wiki/Japanese History/Japan Today, Huston, pg. /1/26/21

 Confucianism

Social Teaching: Confucius, without a doubt, is one of the world's most excellent teachers. His method was "Socratic." His influence on teaching is one of the utmost single intellectual forces among one-quarter of the world's population. His collection of saying so patently didactic, so pedestrian that they often appear typical glance to be one of history's is standing puzzles of wisdom teaching. Note: taken from Huston, pg. 102

The problem Confucius had from eighth high to the third century B.C. was the Dynasty ordering power was progressively deteriorating. Rival barons ranged unchecked, and their unending produced political was in Confucius time. Warfare descended to the unrestrained horror of the Period of the Warring States. The question, "How can they refrain from destroying themselves? Note: taken from Huston, pg. 103

To answer the question, Confucius placed it from a historical perspective. One significantly evolved to keep the community stable, and these ways catch on. Once their patterns are in place, they are transmitted from generation to generation unthinkingly –"cum lactate," sweet and pleasant. Still, traditional society's function. However, few people in China on that day would have paid any attention to tradition. Note: taken from Huston, pg. 103-104

Tradition is the strength of a nation, but people do not respond when it loses its power, and human life faces the greatest crisis it can encounter. Different theories proposed to solve this dilemma, but in most cases, they have failed. For example, the Enlightenment proposed reason; educate citizens, inform them, and count on them to behave sensibly.

A group of thinkers called Realists thought severe punishment would deter infractions would prevent citizens from breaking society's laws. Crime still prevailed. Another implementation of love was another approach to the social problem proposed by "Mo Ti," who advocated the opposite of force. Nevertheless, love does not pay in an inconceivable world. (25 Huston, pg. 106) The Realists' force could restrain gross misconduct, but it would not change attitudes. Mo Ti was closer to the mark in recognizing that attitudes had to change, but Confucius's total reliance on love was unrealistic. Note: taken from Huston, pg. 107

Confucius looked in a different direction to resolve the social ills China was experiencing. He became obsessed with tradition and its power to civilize. Confucius reflected on history and ran across a time in China's history. There was indeed a golden age in China. The Age of the Grand Harmony followed the traditional way of life that their ancestors had perfected and transmitted to their successors.

Principle of Tolerance and Social Responsibility

Confucianism shifted this method of tolerance and social responsibility to liberate every thought to everything. The compatriots needed first to decide what values they wanted to move into place and then turn every education as formal and informal, womb to tomb - to see that universally could internalize. He used moral ideas imparted by every reasonable means, temples, theatres, homes, toys, proverbs, scholarly - until they became habits of the heart. Note: taken from Huston, pg. 109

Confucius Corpus: Confucian project means that humankind's goal is becoming more completely human. The five ongoing relationships present themselves as stable currents in atmospheric conditions than in other respects. As a metaphor for the Confucian project, it introduced an eagle's image that ascends by adjusting its wings to the five stable relationships' currents. The expansion of the eagle wings proceeds in concentric circles that begin with oneself and spread from there to include, successively, one's family, one's face-to-face community, one's nation, and finally, all.

Confucian's five Constant Relationships present themselves as stable currents in atmospheric conditions that, in other respects, can fluctuate wildly. All five are asymmetrical in that (as we have seen) behavior appropriate to one person in each pair differs from what is suitable for the partner. Jen defines the [1] [ideal] relationship that should pertain between individuals – [2] translated as goodness, [three] men to men-ness, [b]enevolence, and [5] love. Display in public life the capacity to "measure the feelings of others by believing that "All men are brothers." Note: taken from Huston pg. 113

Doctrine of Mean

1. Chun Tzu refers to the supreme person and humanity at its best. The mature person is as faithful a rendering as anyone is. How can I accommodate you?
2. There are two ideas to show respect, how things and people's social roles in society. Nothing is more important than father and mother, and self-ruler.
3. The means of power are looked at as rulers. They need the voluntary cooperation of their subjects that emerge when people believe that their leaders merit their collaboration; to give merit,

its leaders must be a person of character devoted to the common good and possess good character that compels respect.
4.   Wen refers to the art of peace compared to music, poetry, and painting, the sum of culture in its aesthetic and spiritual mode.

Ethics or Religion: Confucius used the term transcendent dimension to divide people in the world into a place of heaven and a class of earth, though distinct and solidly joined. Heaven populated the ancestors (ti) as resided over the supreme ancestor Shag Ti. Earth is where mortals currently walk its face. The whole was one unbroken procession in which death signified no more than a transition from the body to an honorable estate. Of the two realms, Heaven is the more powerful, and essential. Note Huston, pg. 116

Being mutually dependent, heaven and the 'earth needed to stay connected, and the best way the world could communicate with heaven was through sacrifice. Augury, too, was another way earth and heaven could stay in touch. Divination was the channel through which earth could tap into what the ancestors could bestow in return – most notably their knowledge of the entire past, which put them in a favorable position to extrapolate what the future held. Early Chinses religious features are its continuity with the ancestors, its sacrifices, and its prophecy. The emphasis was on heaven, the most important of the two terms. Note: taken from Huston, pg. 116

Confucius's religious attention focused more on earth than the Chinese's religion-focused more on heaven. He used concrete instances to shift attention from heaven to the world. For example, which should come; the first claims of earthlings or ancestors? He said, He "recognized that you know what you know and that you are ignorant of what you do not know," he advised. "Hear much, leave to one side that which is doubtful, and speak with due caution concerning the remainder." Note: taken from Huston, pg. 116

Confucius remarks on serving the dead's spirits, he answered, if you cannot help people. How can you fill the soul?" Moreover, when asked about death, he replied, "You do not yet understand life. How can you understand death?" He also shifted attention from ancestor worship to filial piety. Confucius did not interrupt ancestral rites by denying that the spirits of the dead exist. He advised treating them 'as if they were present." He directed his emphasis, though, toward the living family. Note: taken from Huston, pg. 117

The thought Confucius reserved was about the supernatural. He was not without it. Somewhere in the universe, he believed, there is power on the side of the right. It follows from this that the spread of righteousness is a cosmic demand. He taught that heaven's will is the first thing "a Chum Tzu" will respect, and if not, he believed that would back his mission. He said heaven has appointed him to teach his doctrines and until he has done so, people need him to do so. He also said, there is heaven – it knows me. Besides, "He who offends the Gods has no one to pray to." (25 Huston pg. 124)

道   Taoism

Daoism spelled Taoism, an Indigenous religion-philosophical tradition that has shaped Chinese life for more than 2,000 years. In the broadest sense, a Daoist attitude toward life is seen in the accepting and yielding, joyful and carefree sides of the Chinese character, an attitude that offsets and complements the moral and duty-conscious, austere, and purposeful character ascribed to Confucianism. A positive and active attitude characterizes Daoism. It is toward the occult and metaphysical (theories on the nature of reality). In contrast, the agnostic, pragmatic Confucian tradition considers only marginal importance. Although such issues exist, Confucianism in China seeks to balance them and Taoism. The word means path or way. There are three senses in which Taoism explains its theory.

Three Meanings of Taoism: First, Taoism is the way of ultimate reality. Toa cannot perceive or even clearly conceive, for it is too vast for a reason to be a fathom. In the second sense, it is the universe's way; the norm, the rhythm, and the driving power in all nature. Spirit, rather than matter, cannot be exhausted because the more it is drawn upon, the more it flows. In its third sense, Tao refers to the way of human life when it meshes with the Tao of the universe just described. Note: taken from Huston, pg. 117

Three Approaches to Power & Taoism: Tao Te Ching, the title of Taoism's introductory text, translated as The Way and It Powers, and the three ways to approach power. Taoism's three genera in China are so unlike that they first saw there is no unity with each other. Identifying each starts with two have the standard designation.

Philosophical Taoism and Religious or Popular Taoism: First order is religious. The second order is the third school is too heterogeneous to have acquired a single appointment. The populations constitute an identifiable cluster by sharing a common objective. All were engaged in vitalizing programs intended to facilitate the Tao's power, its Te, as it flows through human beings. Note: taken from Huston, pg. 1126-27

Philosophical Taoism (Efficient Power): Philosophical is not a church but a self-help program. The leaders are teachers or coaches who train students or tell students what they should be doing. They are philosophical or vitalizing teachers who instruct what students should understand or what they should do. Both of these teachers teach in camps, telling the students to work by themselves. Note: taken from Huston, pg. 128

Philosophical Taoism is an attitude toward life. Its link established is with powering through remembering; philosophy sees knowledge, and that knowledge is power. The experience that Taoism teaches; expertise and capabilities of life; what can be called wisdom. Live wisely to live in a way that conserves life's vitality by not expending it in useless, draining ways. The chief of these draining life living is friction and conflict, but to live the Taoism way in pure effectiveness. Action in Wu Wei's mode activated in which clash – in interpersonal relationships, in "intrapsychic conflict" and concerning nature – is reduced to the minimum. Note: taken from Huston, pg. 128-129

Taoist Hygiene & Yoga (Augmented Power): The word ch'i provides the proper entrance to this second school of thought, for though it means breath but means vital energy. Taoists used it to refer to the Tao's power that they experienced coursing through them – or not coursing because it was blocked. Taoist main objective is to remove the obstacles that reduced the flow of energy. Ch'i says power is a delight – for authority is the life force, and the Taoists love life. To be alive is good; to be happening is better; to be always alive is best. Note: taken from Huston, pg. 130

Taoism used three ways to maximize ch'i, matter, movement, and the. Respecting matter, they tried eating things and discovered a remarkable pharmacopeia of medicinal herbs. The efforts to extract Ch'i from the case into its stable, a liquid. A gaseous form: supplemented by bodily movement programs such as t'ai-chi to invite ch'i from the cosmos and remove blocks to its internal flow. The mind contemplatives developed Taoist mediation. Increasing ch'i through meditation is the most subtle and enquires long treatment. Note: taken from Huston, pg. 130

Meditational Taoism arose as the advancing self-consciousness of the Chinese brought the subjective experience to full view. Novel and noteworthy, this world of the inner self-invited exploration given directly as the source of one's awareness was a momentous experience for one then saw 'the self as meant to be.' One saw not merely "things perceived," but "that by which we perceive," It was to reach the pure perception that Taoist yogis meditated. Note: take from Huston, pg. 131

The Chinese social preoccupation led them to press the possibility that the ch'i poured into yogis when their minds emptied of self-seeking. Disturbing emotions and distracting thoughts that could be transmitted supernaturally to the community enhance its vitality and harmonize its affairs. The powers that could be thus acquired and redirected "could shift Heaven and earth." In the condition of total inactivity and stillness, the heart and mind were open as never before to the Tao. "To the mind that is still the whole universe surrenders." Note: taken from Huston, pg. 131

Religious Taoism (Vicarious Power): Religious Taoism is a full-fledged church. Taoism institutionalized psychics, shamans, faith healers, and soothsayers in the second century A. D. into a church. Its pantheon consists of Loa Tzu and two other deities, and the texts issued from them came accepted without question. The line of succession in this church continues down to the present in Taiwan. Note: taken from Huston, pg. 132

The Taoism priesthood text used is to pack the descriptions of rituals that have magical effects if exactly performed. The word magic holds the key to this priestly version of Taoism. Much of religious Taoism deals with energy, which looks like crude superstition. One historian puts it this way, the Taoism priesthood made cosmic life-power available for ordinary villagers." The rubric of magic is a tradition of the Taoism Church. It was divided into freelance wizards, exorcists, and shamans, which devised ways to harness higher powers for humane ends. Note: taken from Huston, pg. 133

Taoist Vitalizing Programs: Philosophical Taoism vitalized programs for increasing one's chi and the Taoism church. The three programs initiated were concerned with maximizing the Tao's animating Te but later became specifics concerns. The specifics of their problems fall to a continuum. The continuum begins with an interest in how the usual life allotment of ch'i can deploy to affect philosophical Taoism better. From there, it moved on to ask if that average quotient could increase using Taoist vitalizing programs. Finally, Taoism believed that cosmic energy was fathered into people through burning glass. They then transmitted to the ones who needed it, and to whom are the ones who could not get it on their enacting with Religious Taoism. Note: taken from Huston, pg. 134

The danger in this arrangement is that the lines between them are not concrete walls and separate them in the interest of clarity. However, throughout history, each has interacted with the other two, right down to Taoism in Hong King and Taiwan today, it is rare to find a Taoist not involved with all their school.

CHAPTER IV
RELIGIONS OF THE
MIDDLE EAST

Judaism

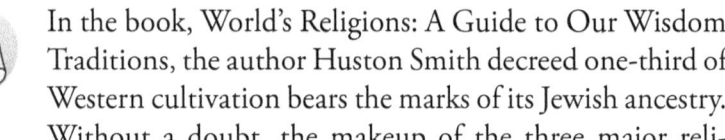 In the book, World's Religions: A Guide to Our Wisdom Traditions, the author Huston Smith decreed one-third of Western cultivation bears the marks of its Jewish ancestry. Without a doubt, the makeup of the three major religions travels through many critical areas of Africa and the beliefs of the Middle East of Europe bearing the meaning of God. Through their collections of other religions' purpose of God, they put together their understanding of whom, what, and why God existence, and His relationship to humanity. [8]

The Jewish collections of the Supreme Being passed down through history gave the Western region of the world its most excellent religion that expressed God's meaning. The author's real impact on the ancient Jews lies in the content to which Western civilization took over the perspective on the most profound questions life poses the passion for the meaning of God. Note: taken from Smith, pg. 180

Belief in One God: Monotheism is the belief in a single God. The Jewish quest centered on their understanding of the Supreme Being. Their acceptance of faith in a Greater Being than themselves took them far from the self-center self and their sense of power. Next, he said the glory of the One God's meaning took away any alternative connections. In this, they were at one with their ancient equals. Note: taken from Smith, pg. 180

The Jewish people's supreme achievement of the religion came in three ways. First, they tended to be amoral. The people's unethical side always presented the illusion of why the Great God would visit and protect such people. Next, they had no concerns about human beings' matters, but their pursuit was to know the ways of God. The Hebrew method of meaning continued from Abraham's path, Promise's ancestor, to become a great nation. The Promise given to him was his offspring would be numerous as the stars are in the sky. Note: taken from Smith, pg. 180

The Meaning of Creation: The book of Genesis starts with Adam and Eve. They are the first created man and woman that changed the face of life for them and all creation. They disobeyed God's instructions not to eat from the tree of knowledge of good and evil, or they will surely die, which they did along with the entire human race. Their act changed the face of living for the whole of human beings. The man and woman's disobedient act caused them to leave the preemptive ground prepared for them and live a life, not in harmony with God. The entire theme of the first five books of the Old Testament seemed to shout stop sinning and live for God. Note: taken from Smith, pg. 180

Islam

Allah's movement: With a few striking exceptions, Islam's basic theological concepts are identical to those of Judaism and Christianity, its forerunners. Islam starts with God co-creating with earth and after it, human beings. The name of the first man was Adam. Adam and Eve's descendants led to Noah, who had a son named Shem, from which the word Semite derives. The descendants of Shem led to Abraham, who married Sarah. Sarah had no son, so Abraham took Hagar for his second wife. Hagar bore him a son, Ishmael, after that Sarah conceived and likewise had a son, named Isaac. Sarah demanded Abraham banish Ishmael and Hagar from the tribe because Hagar mocked her because she now airs to Abraham. The Koran follows the Bible, but here the accounts diverge, for according to the Koran, Ishmael went to the place where Mecca was to rise. His descendants, flourishing in Arabia, became Muslims, whereas Isaac, who remained in Palestine, gave rise to the

Hebrews who called themselves Jews. Note: taken from Smith, pgs. 148-157

Allah: The word Allah means God, for there is only one God. In Muslims' eyes, Islam begins not with Muhamad in sixth-century Arabia, but with God. In the beginning, God. The book of Koran, name of God is Allah. Note: taken from Smith, pg. 146

Muhammad: Muhammad was born into Mecca's leading tribe, the Koreish, and was named Muhammad, "highly praised." The angels of God opened Muhammad's heart and filled it with light. The description epitomizes his early character as this comes down to tradition. Pure-hearted and beloved in his cycle, he said a sweet and gentle disposition. His grief, having made him sensitive to human suffering in every form, was always ready to help, incredibly the weak and the poor. Note: taken from Smith, pg. 148

Belief in One God: Creation-Evolution: According to the Merriam-Webster Dictionary, the word Theosis means faith in one God as the creator and ruler of the universe, without rejection of evolution. The term theism derives from the Greek word Theos or the meaning "god." The term theism first used by Ralph Cudworth (1617–1688). In Cudworth's definition, theosis is "strictly and properly called Theists, who affirm that a perfectly conscious understanding being, or mind, existing of itself from eternity, was the cause of all other things." [A1]

Another theory of that meaning comes from Thoreau. It means one who moves fluidly between the two, shuttling between the divine and the here-and-now, between theism and materialism. The problem lies with the choice of man's meaning of materialism. The earth and the universe have a maker, or it develop by chance, from a single cell organism that evolved into existence.

Second, the belief in evolution leaves out God. Science views the beginning of materialism evolved through cycles of change over some time. There is no reality of God creating the world and its inhabitants.

Zoroastrianism (Baha'i)

 One of the world's continued practices of religion is Zoroastrianism or Mazdayasna. A multi-faceted faith centered on a dualistic cosmology of good and evil and an eschatology predicting evil's ultimate conquest with theological elements of henotheism, monotheism/monism, and polytheism. The religion recognizes the teachings of Iranian-speaking spiritual leader Zoroaster (also known as Zarathustra). The religion exalts an uncreated and benevolent deity of wisdom, Ahura Mazda (Wise Lord), as its supreme being. Zoroastrianism's historical features, such as messianism, judgment after death, heaven, and hell, and free will, may have influenced other religious and philosophical systems such as Judaism, Greek philosophy, Christianity, Islam, the Bahá'í Faith, and Buddhism.

Today the number of Zoroastrian followers is small, and most live in India, Iran, and North America. Zoroaster proclaimed that Ahura Mazda was the supreme creator, the creative and sustaining force of the universe through Asha. Human beings are given the right to choose between supporting Ahura Mazda or not, making them responsible for their choices.

Zoroastrianism is not uniform in theological and philosophical thought, especially with historical and modern influences having a significant impact on individual and local beliefs, practices, values, and vocabulary, sometimes merging with tradition and in other cases displacing it. Modern Zoroastrianism, however, tends to divide itself into either Reformist or Traditionalist camps with various smaller movements arising. In Zoroastrianism, life's purpose is to become an Ashavan (a master of Asha) and bring happiness into the world, contributing to the cosmic battle against evil.

Zoroastrianism's core teachings include:

- Follow the Threefold Path of Asha: Humata, Huxta, Huvarshta (good thoughts, right words, and virtuous deeds).
- The charity maintains the soul-aligned to Asha and spreads happiness.

- The spiritual equality and duty of genders. Being suitable for the sake of goodness and without the hope of reward

Christianity

 To become a Christian, one must believe that God sent his Son Jesus Christ, to die on the cross to forgive the universe of sin instilled in them because of the first man Adam's disobedience. God gave His Son Jesus as a sacrifice to redeem humankind from the powers of the enemy, who is Satan, a powerful spiritual being that teaches hearers of his words that every Word of God is false. One must be baptized in the Name of Jesus and receive the Holy Spirit to empower him and guild him into all truth.

Christianity is faith teaching about God and living a moral life. The instructions that are derived are from the Holy Bible. The religious outlook is to teach the world about the gift of the salvation of God. They believe all humanity lacks the power to live a pleasing life to God because of sins. The utterly human race resides in a sinful body that Jesus eradicated when God came in human form as Jesus Christ.

God defeated Satan's rule over the minds of humanity. Humanity has the power to leave sinless lives when empowered with the Holy Spirit of God, which is the gift of Salvation. Salvation is the tool that makes heaven a reality in the lives of believers. It makes it possible for them to experience the power of God and enables them to live a life pleasing to God. The good news is to tell the next person about the Salvation of God, a free and life-changing gift.

FINAL REMARKS

 Religion is a powerful tool and a life-changing device in the hearts of humanity. If used right, it can change or be used to better society or make them into slaves. Every practice of humanity can be good or evil, even in religions. It comes down to knowing what the guidelines are that make

up a good religion. Scriptures teach that each individual has to work out his or her salvation. As Christian, they will have to pray and read their Bible to understand Christianity fully.

Jesus also said he had other sheep besides the sheep He counseled, and He told the disciples to spread the gospels of the good news about Jesus. Looking through most religions, I saw some portions of the good news had reached others across the world. Culture tends to dominate religion. Therefore, one has to work out their own religious belief with fear before the Lord. Paul, a Christian, said I come to show you a more excellent way to worship God.

REFERENCES

1.   Smith, Huston. *World's Religions*, HarperCollins Publications: New York, NY, 1994
https://www.britannica.com/place/India/History (1/7/21)
2.   Esposito, John L., Fasching, Darrell J., and Lewis, Todd. World Religions today, Oxford University Press: New York, NY, 2009
3.   Richard, Spann J. The Christian Faith and Secularism, New York, NY: Abingdon-Cokesbury Press,
Notes: Smith, Huston. New York, NY: HarperCollins Publishers, 1994

the WORLD OF RELIGIONS ends

PART III

EXPERTS DISCUSS THE EFFECTS ON HUMAN BEHAVIORS

CHAPTER I
INQUIRIES

In most cases, the influence of the human mind's good or evil power can be useful or hostile. The concept of good and evil comes from religion. The idea of righteousness and sin is looked at as a fight for the souls of humankind. It is an argument between the forces of God and the forces of Satan. Non-religious theories of good and bad are about the conduct of humanity. Both approaches affirm humankind has a good and evil nature.

The inquiries about each subject of the discussions gave insight into the type of questions asked. The methods of probes used were to evoke the reasons behind the arguments. The inquiries lessen the tension between the two different subjects. One or two examinations of the subject performed and answered were to start the discussions.

The first inquiry was about what makes God - God? The investigation searched through many religions to see the difference in the way people worship and serve God to know the significance in their lives because they believed in Him. The research continued the inquiry about living a secular life as opposed to a religious one. Questions asked what benefits are rewarded for living a spiritual life-style in comparison to living a secular lifestyle.

The next inquiry sided up the public schools and examined the no discipline rule to see students' behaviors. The question used biblical disciplines and secular restraint of discipline as doing good and no harm and determined which one produced the best action in students. The inquiry went further and asked how punishment harms students and whether it positively or negatively changes their behaviors.

The third inquiry discussed the effects of civil obedience. Why is civil obedience a challenge as inhuman treatment? What consideration is the cruel treatment when people who commit crimes are disciplined for their evil acts? Moreover, civil obedience design is more of a disciplinary punishment than corrective or rehabilitation programs to correct civil disobedience. The inquiry examined the concept of freedom of choice and bondage theory to see the difference in the two views to explore the approaches of cause and effect and God's Salvation.

The fourth inquiry asked the question. If people evolved, then there is no God. The search went further to see the difference in the theories of creation and evolution.

The fifth and final inquiry asked why to live extraordinary and honest lives when everybody else lives to survive. The question asks why God made hell, and evil people will live there for eternity after death. Does sending people to a place of torment called hell because of their disobedient lifestyle of sinful living make God a good or evil God?

Discuss Inquiries

The five discussion questions selected were from the inquiries. The five queries were formally from authors who have authored books about the subjects. The Bible is used extensively to rebuttal the opposition's responses. In most of the discussions, the questions addressed were about the world's ways of living compared to holy living.

First Discussion
Why Believe in God?

The Name of God is found in all cultures around the world. The very definition of God gives an account that He is the only God. The illustration offers titles to His characteristics, deity, and attributes that say He is God. The proofs of God's existence are found in words that give tribute to his supremacy were discussed. Experts agreed, and many disagreed that the theory of God is correct.

Second Discussion
Should love given over punishment
when a person acts evil?

Love and punishment are compassions of the human desires to set things right or divulge the wrongs. The theory of love means that love supersedes all other evils, and the punishment is supposed to do the same, but the problem between the two, love, forgives. Punishment is a correction that was discussed. How are they related to justice?

Third Discussion
When does humanity' have freedom
of choice? Is that real freedom?

When humanity's will be free, then there is freedom, or when humanity's choice is open, then there is bondage. What are the ingredients for people to have self-will or live in captivity? What are the causes that make people act good or evil? Is it because of cause and effect or influences of the mind's commands to perform good or bad behaviors? Do people have the will to choose?

Fourth Discussion
Can the Wonder of Human Design be Explained?

Is it possible for the dead to come back to life and live again? The discussion centered on the death and resurrection of Jesus Christ.

Fifth Discussion
The Problem with Evil, and is there hell?

The discussion presented the theory of good and evil; can they go hand and hand? What are the meaning and effects of heaven and hell?

CHAPTER II
DISCUSSIONS

Discussion I

Theologian and Philosopher Discussed, Why Believe there Is a God?

William Paley used his Design Theory from his book "A View of the Evidence of Christianity" (1794) to discuss that a Supreme Being created nature. He used the human eye as an example. He affirmed God's existence because of the design of nature. The wonders surrounding humanity are unspeakable and cannot be explained with human intellect; therefore, only the ideal of supreme intelligence could have designed such a phenomena.

The Argument for the Theory of Design

Paley used the human eye to support his theory. He said that it is impossible for the human eye just to happen. The human eye is perfectly designed to function as a looking glass for the body. Only one part is missing from the eye; the eye would not work correctly. He said there is no reason to disagree with Design Theory. Therefore, God created the human body and the universe.

Paley's Premises: Either the wonders of nature occurred randomly, by chance, or they are the product of an intelligent designer. They could not have happened by chance. Therefore, they are the work of a superior designer.

Problem with Design Theory: Some critics see fault with Design Theory. They said the Design Theory has no reference to its background because it is missing. The background information would license the Design Theory. Even though God is the creator of the existence (universe), the lack of inference makes it impossible to verify the cause or the evidence that He is the creator.

Response: The lack of reference is not an excellent reason for a good fault in the Design Theory. It is not the evidence of the authority that is being questioned, but the evidence that nature could not have happened by chance. Moreover, the human eye's makeup and performance designed by an intelligent supreme intellect is the only possible solution. It is impossible for them and all of existence just to have appeared. Therefore, it must be a supreme being that created all presence and created it for a reason.

Notes: Taken from Problems from Philosophy, pgs. 11-15

An opponent of the Design Theory

David Hume (1711-1776) disagreed with the Design Theory. His argument is taken from his book Dialogue Concerning Natural Religions, Published in 1779. He exposed the weakness of the Design Theory showing a flaw in the designer. He said the idea that the world was made by a "single-all-powerful, all-good deity does not seem plausible." The entire universe (world) is not perfect. In addition, he said, "people are justified in believing in God, even though they could never know God's presence empirically."

Response: It might seem that the entire universe is not perfect, but the design is perfect. God designed nature to support humanity, given that without it, society could not exist. Therefore, it is plausible that there had to be a superior intelligent designer knowledgeable enough to design nature just for humanity to live on the earth.

Is God a Supreme Being? Even though God does not live among human beings or interact with them, He does exist when humans interact with him. The very definition of God clarifies his existence. His signature of creation of all things tells of his presence, and the acts of nature express His glorious attributes. God might not be a visible reality for humanity to see, but his signature is seen in their minds, throughout the world, and in the universe.

According to Random House Webster's Dictionary, [A1] God is a Supreme Being that created the universe, the world, and its habitations. God's creations are one of a kind, and no other being can reproduce them exactly as he did. For example, take the tree. It is a marvelously created thing of beauty and bears green leaves, but a tree's principal purpose is to give off oxygen for humankind to breathe. Therefore, without the existence of the tree, humanity could not live on earth.

The Rebuttal for the Existence of God: Peter van Inwagen a philosopher who converted to Christianity, wrote, "If the universe is not self-sustained," then it could not exist by itself. Then the universe must be sustained by something, and that something must be God. He argued for the existence of God is necessary. He said the God of necessity would not fail to exist because He must sustain the universe.

He Formulated a First Cause Argument: The universe is a dependent thing. It cannot exist by itself; it can only exist if sustained by something that is not dependent. God, a necessary being, is the only thing that is not dependent. Therefore, God supports the universe. Note: Taken from Problems from Philosophy, pgs. 23-24

Discussion II

Jesus, various religions, and non-religions debated over whether love should be given and not punishment when people act uncivilly. Jesus used scriptures to show the first two most important commandments: to love God with all your heart and soul and love your neighbor as yourself.

The argument for Love is Justice

God's love is felt in all hearts of humankind, and it is spoken in many different languages and revealed in many different concepts and ways. Although the idea of God's love applied differently to humanity's lives, it still shows his love and justice. The love of God revealed through the teachings of Jesus Christ showed justice. One of humankind's virtues is to show love and not judge each other.

Hinduism Response: In Hinduism, the love of God is associated with Kiruna, who shows compassion and mercy, which impels one to help reduce the suffering of others. Bhakti is a Sanskrit term, sense loving devotion to the supreme God. Hinduism's mystic side takes Yoga forms that include "Ishvarapranidhana, or self-surrender to God, and his worship." [1] In other words, Hinduism says to act justly to be right and show love, not to judge.

Christianity Response: In Christianity, the love of God in Jeremiah 31:2 expresses, "I have loved you with an everlasting love; I have drawn you with loving-kindness." [A1] Jesus showed the love of God on the cross when he was being crucified. "He said, "Father forgives them, for they know not what they do." He said to act justly to be right and show love, not to judge. Cited from Jeremiah 31:3 [A2]

Islamic Response: The love of God is the foundation of the Islamic religion. They show the love of God in prayer, in reference, and fear to show honor and to show respect toward God. Muslims to show the love of Allah, they show love to one another. Another Islamic concept of God's love is to lean toward the performance of honorable deeds. For example, a good deed is to feed the needy with food. This showed the love of God when virtuous deeds are performed. In other words, they act justly to be right and show love, not to judge.

Judaism Response: Judaism uses the scriptures in Deuteronomy to show humanity to show the love for God, which is the "essence of Judaism." [8] And you shall love the Lord your God with all your heart and with all your soul and with all the might." In other words, the words of Judaism just act justly to be right and show love, not to judge. Notes: Cited from Deuteronomy 6:5 [A2]

Still, the contrast where love and justice met displayed in Micah 6:8 showed that love is compatible with justice. The Psalmist said, "O man, what is right and what does the Lord require of you, for you to act justly and to show love, mercy and to walk humbly before Him. In addition, Jesus said he did not come to change the Law but to fulfill it.

The argument for how Justice is Love

The Law of God: Jesus said humankind is to love God first, and they are to love one another. Jesus' unlimited messages were about the love of God and the love of each other. The love message He preached was love is justice. For example, when the woman is caught in adultery, he said anyone without sin throws the first rock. Another love message he gave was when he was hanging on the ground and being crucified. He asked God to forgive them, for he said; they know not what they do. Cited from Mark 12:29-34 [A2]

However, he did not hesitate to make things right that were wrong when He had to go up against evil.

Rebuttal gives Punishment instead of Love: The ethical doctrine of Utilitarianism axiom believes that the "greatest happiness of the most significant number should be the criterion of the virtue of action." [2] The argument for punishment should be used only as far as it "promotes general happiness." [2]

They said yes, using punishment, and only if it prevents offenders from doing further harm, is used as a deterrent to prevent recidivism, and discourages other potential offenders. It gives satisfaction to victims and society. Moreover, it is used to reform offenders and to help them become productive members of society

Kant responded to the utilitarianism theory of greatest happiness: Immanuel Kant (1724 – 1804) was a German philosopher and one of the central Enlightenment thinkers. For Kant, punishment is giving criminals what they deserve is the only legitimate reason to punish them. "If we punish them for promoting happiness, then we are violating the categorical imperative by treating them as a mere means to an end. So, all of the practical justifications for punishment are bad ones, according to Kant." [3]

His theory of punishment is "commonly regarded as purely retributive in nature." [3] Punishment is a warning intended to deter crime. It was a tool in civil society's hands to counteract human drives toward violating another's rights. However, in its execution, the state was limited in its reaction by a retributive theory of justice demanding respect for the individual as an end and not as a means of prevention to further social goals.

Love, punishment, and justice appear not to interact with each other. Love is given, and the giver expects it to be given back. Love means showing kindness. Not so with discipline. Discipline is used with the expectation it will change for the better that individual or limit their destructive behaviors toward society. Both are given in love, but the outcomes are different. Justice, in both cases, means it is allocated relatively, not so with punishment or love.

Discussion III

A theologian, humanist, Philosopher, and psychologist debated what entitles the freedom of humanity's will. They asked the question; what constitutes real freedom of the intention of humanity?

They debated controversial questions about the bondage of humanity's will or their will to be free. Martin Luther wrote many hypotheses to show how God had vindicated the bandage over humanity's will over Satan's rule. He said the bondage of the intention of society is their sins. However, human philosophers and psychologists disagreed with Martin Luther's theory of free will. Still, others respond positively. Even so, the two scholars, in particular, objected to his solution of the bondage of the free will of humanity. One, in particular, was Erasmus of Rotterdam.

Martin Luther (1483-1546)

Martin Luther presented his theology of the "free will" [10] to discuss the essence of God's love toward humanity. He argued God wills all events in life. Predestination explains the fate of the individual soul, which addresses the "paradox of free will." [10]

He explained the power Satan had over the souls of humanity that Jesus interceded.

Luther said the influences of evil stop people from working out their salvation, making it impossible to choose a suitable response over evil. They can be completely free of their sinful nature and possess the will to bring them to obtain the salvation of God to be completely free from Satan's rule over their lives.

Erasmus of Rotterdam (1466-1536)

Desiderius Erasmus (1469-1536), a Dutch humanist, was one of the northern Renaissance Period's most excellent scholars. He disagreed with Martin Luther's theory of the bondage of the free will of human beings. He said God had endowed humanity with free will is a valuable trait found in all humans. Their free will is theirs to be rewarded or punished according to their right and bad choices. He argued that the vast majority of the biblical texts explicitly supported this view, and that divine grace was how humans became aware of God, as well as the force that sustained and motivated humans as they sought out their own free will to follow God's laws or Satan's.

Response: Both theories are right. They just addressed different assumptions. Luther preached God's salvation that broke Satan's bond over humanity's choice, which gave humanity the free will to choose and live according to his gift of Salvation. Humanity's free will is possible because of Jesus Christ's sacrifice to win over human's sinful nature from Satan. He eradicated Satan's rule over their character. Erasmus declared society could choose between good and evil; no evil forces can stop them, but he lacks redemptive knowledge to see Satan's real powers and God's gift of Salvation.

Argument of Determinist

Philosophers see the theory of determinism as different from religious determinism. Determinism sees humanity in a relationship with God's omniscience causing them to be incompatible with their free will. In this discussion, he regarded Luther's theory of predestination as a form of religious determinism. Cited from Problems from Philosophy, pg. 117-118

Jesus told his hearers that they needed to be made "free indeed" (John 8:36). He said to them that if they followed him, he would teach them how to live a life of freedom from bondage to sin. Humanity now has the power to control sinful nature and live a god-fearing lifestyle, but only if they choose to. Being free indeed comes through the power of the Holy Spirit, changing humanity's sinful nature. This is what freedom of bandage means, not being controlled under Satan's influence is but able to decide to make good choices.

On the other hand, determinism agreed that the laws of nature are in control of this world. They said everything happens governed by invariable laws of cause and effect. People are the product of forces that shape their lives. People have no control over their choices or actions. Cited from Problems from Philosophy, pg. 117-118

Determinism Theory goes like this … Everything people do cause by forces over which they have no control. If their actions are driven by forces over which they have no control, they do not act freely. Thus, they never act freely. Cited from Problems from Philosophy; pg. 118

Psychologists agreed with the theory of determinism. It reveals the human character shaped by an individual's genes and the environment. However, what about individuals' responsibilities? The above remarks and the illustration are what the psychologist used to defend their side of the discussion. They presented two men who had committed a crime and went to prison. One lived a life bereft of non-affection killed in jail, and the other was released to gain employment helping other people. The theory of determinism agreed that both individuals lived by the hands dealt.

The response of Libertarians: Libertarianism disagrees with determinism theory. They say yes, the laws of cause and effect determine precisely what will happen, but a human decision is not like that. The rules of cause and effect do not have control over a person's choice. The assumption is not liable. People can reason in each situation before finalizing their decision.

Discussion IV

A philosopher and a theologian discussion - Is it possible for the dead to come back to life and live again?

David Hume's Argument against Miracles

David Hume (1711-1776) authored articles on naturalism, an effective philosophical empiricism system, and skepticism. In his book *A Treatise of Human Nature* (1739–40), he argued against the existence of innate ideas, positing that all human knowledge derives solely from experience. Hume argued that inductive reason and belief in causality could not be justified rationally; instead, they result from habits of the mind.

In another book, *An Inquiry Concerning Human Understanding* (1748), he claimed a need to induce reason to draw any causal inferences from experiences. If the future is predicted, then an experience must have happened in the past. It is necessary to presuppose that the future will resemble the past, a presupposition proven in a prior experience.

In his book, he made scandalous remarks about religion and morals. He did not object to miracles' display, but his objection was that there is no reason to believe in them. He used examples to argue that if someone says a dead man came back to life, can that statement be counted as accurate or believed? First, the belief with probability that it could have happened (right), or it could not have occurred (false)

In other words, that person implied that the event was more likely not to have occurred. Then, the false hood of his testimony would be more miraculous than the possibility that there are no known cases of someone truly dead coming back to life and living among the living. If a reasonable person quoted a statement, the report would have to be a downside from its original claim. Therefore, the claim that miracles are related to people returning to life after experiencing death is not practicable. Moreover, the event is impossible to formulate. Cited from Problems from Philosophy pgs. 54-55

Arguments for Miracles

The definition of a miracle is when a person claimed he saw something, or something happened that is unlikely to have seen or happened. Miracles are reported when a person has an incurable disease that will cause him or her to die. The person said that he received a holy man's prayer, and the condition disappeared, and miraculous healing was reported to the physician who said the phenomena might have occurred. Notes: A physician sees a miracle: https://www.christianhealingmin.org/index.php/hl-issue-2010-5/204-magazine/2006-2010/hl-articles-2010-5/394-a-physician-sees-a-miracle

Rebuttal for the Argument Against Miracles: For David Hume's theory of miracles to be irrelevant, he would have had to become a believer and experience Christianity. Therefore, he cannot say miracles are all irrelevant. He has no reference for claiming people cannot return from the dead to life.

The argument for the Resurrection of Jesus Christ

First, to finalize the death and reincarnation of Jesus Christ, a historical analysis formulated a reason. The prophecy that a child would be born to take away humanity's sins is predicted in the Old Testament. An unbeliever would never understand the child's significance of being born, called Emmanuel, meaning God with us.

A miracle occurred that caused God to come into the world. He prepared a human body to live in. Scripture spoke of another blessing when a virgin gave birth without having intercourse with a man, but this could only happen because she was over shallowed with the Holy Spirit, another miracle. From the time of Jesus' birth to his death, there are reports of miracles, miracles, and more miracles. He had miracles of protection, miracles of wisdom, and he performed miracles of healing.

Thus, the reason behind the miracle revealed the sense of the event. Miracles are not supposed to happen, but they are used to formulate a purpose. In this case, the miracle is the resurrection of Jesus from the dead. Three of the many reasons Jesus resurrected from the dead follows:

It is a miracle of Jesus' reincarnated body to gain possession of the dead body to occupy it for the Holy Spirit's entrance. This miracle happened for the Holy Spirit to embody the human body. God cannot dwell in the human body because that is where carnality lives and where sin arises because of the flesh's lust. God is sovereign, and nothing or nobody can dominate his present.

The miracle of Jesus' reincarnation showed the love of God for the human race. God sent his Word in the form of His Son to be a sacrifice to appeal to Satan's request to get back the soul of humanity.

In allowing his Son to be a sacrifice, he retained total control of his creation and time.

The miracle of Jesus' reincarnation caused them to accept the Church into the Body of God. Now the Church can execute the powers of God under the gift of the Holy Spirit. The Spirit works miracles in believers' lives daily, and the church is the ruling authority of the world.

Notes: Historical records revealed that Jesus lived in Jerusalem, he died on the cross, and a miracle happened when he rose from the dead.

Discussion V

Theologians, Psychologists, Sociologists, and Philosophers argued about good and evil. Can they or can they not go hand and hand? Why does humanity choose to live a life of freedom of choice rather than live according to God's law of salvation to enable them to go live eternality in heaven, not live eternality in hell?

The argument for the Proof of the Existence of God

Humanity sees through their eyes, but first, the mind has to shape things into existence. The science of psychology studies and explains human thought and behavior. Their knowledge is based on what they see and on scientific facts. In most cultures, people believe God exists, but science, in most cases, finds it hard to confirm his presence. They say there are not enough references to his being of existence.

God and the Origin of the Universe: First, there are two theories about the origin of the universe that humanity can believe that brought it into existence: creation or evolution. The first says God created it, and the second says he did not. Therefore, to say the universe's seeable material is not God's creation is to say there is no God.

Second, the universe and its inhabitants exist through humankind's eyes, but they lack the knowledge to explain their position in this vast universe. They are the only beings who can identify and explain how they may have come into existence and how it works. Scientists can tell the future from the experiences of the past. Nevertheless, they have no clue why it is here and why they and all other life forms exist, and the purposes of their existence.

The knowledge of the world: The knowledge about the world, the universe, and humanity are limited. They can only know what they see around them. Theologians used biblical history, and evolutionists used biology to understand life's existence. Sociologists used theories of the interaction of people in their environments. Science is the breakdown of a view to having a method that can predict an event's outcome. The theory is the only science beyond humankind's reasoning, but it cannot answer God's unknown facts about what humanity sees.

How do we survive life after death?

The reality of death happens. However, not an experience of life. The two avenues' people believe are life after death or no life after death. They also believe that another world is real after death, accept its validity, or do not experience it. Death is not preventable, and it happens to all humans. It is not the problem of dying for all who share it, but what about life effects on life after living on earth?

CHAPTER III
FINALIZATION OF
DISCUSSION QUESTIONS

The argument for Why Humanity chose to go to hell rather than decide to go to heaven, the place of eternality?

Theologians explain why people do not believe in God, why they refuse to worship him, and why they will not obey his covenant agreements. They blame God for all the evil in the world, and they said they could not worship a God that allows evil to happen to people. They would rather spend eternity in hell than worship the Almighty God.

Does humanity have another choice of the ruling benefactor that can make their lives a better place other than hell? No, no one has the signature of God except him. God's signature bears the marks of good and righteousness, and if people do not want to go to heaven, they refuse to live a life that honors God's signature. No benefactor besides God has the power to will where a person will go after death except Him.

There are no other words in the human mind that can prevent humanity from going to hell. Jesus tells humankind to choose whether they will spend eternity with him: "Very truly I tell you, whoever hears my word and believes him who sent me has eternal life and will not be judged but has crossed over from death to life" (taken from John 5:24). In John 14:6, Jesus says, "I am the way, the truth, and the life. No one comes to the Father except through me."

Jesus said, "Wide is the gate/broad is the road that leads to destruction, and many enter through it," "But small is the gate, and narrow is the road that leads to life, and only a few find it" (Matthew 7:13). " A2 Just as Moses lifted the snake in the wilderness, so too the Son of Man must be lifted, that everyone who believes may have eternal life in him" (John 3:14-15).A2

FINAL REMARK

 The origins of man came from both theories of creation and evolution. The design tells who did it, and evolution tells the story of the show it came about. It is not so much so or show that is at stake here, but the belief that God exists and can be the author of creating the universe and its inhabitants.

The theory of creation is a traditional and ancient belief in the existence of humanity and its surroundings. It gives a logical solution to existence design, but it lacks the references to prove that it is a creation of intellect more incredible than humanity's mind. However, all facts point to someone, or something created with more advanced intelligence than humankind has. All the odds add up to the earth's intelligent design, and humanity is part of a superior mindset creation.

REFERENCES

1. Esposito, John L., Fasching, Darrell, J & Lewis Todd. World Religions Today, New York, NY: Oxford University Press, Inc., 2009
2. Rachels, James. Problems from Philosophy, New York, NY: McGraw-Hill Companies, 2005
3. Paulson, Steven. Luther for Armchair Theologians, Louisville, KY: Westminster John Knox Press, 2004 Johnston, Jerry. Apostasy Now, Overland Park, Kansas: Jerry Johnston Publishing

the EXPERTS DISCUSS IMPACTS ON
THE HUMAN MIND ends

THE AUTHOR'S NOTES

LIFE LIVING

All of humanity has thought patterns designed to live according to the order of nature governed by God's Laws. When **CONCLUSION** folks believe differently, they create a desire to live a life in which the law & order is set according to their flame of knowledge. So, people who disregard the Knowledge of God, their Creator, and His instructions of life living, which are predesignated what were and designed for them, and all other inhabitants of the world cause a problematic reaction against all creation! Taken from Micah 6:6&8; 7:7 [A2]

Between Life Choices: A Christian should always consider that all choices are one's own opinion. One should live according to the Holy Bible's principles. This gives a positive edge of thinking to understand the principles of right over wrong in a world of backward thinkers.

An alternative way a problem is solved is to look at it in a philosophical setting. Philosophy is religion, when it points to God, but looks at a problem differently than a theologian. However, theology is the basis of a religious belief.

THEOLOGY

 Theologians across the world try to make sense of religion. Every religion has a fundamental belief about God that the unseen supernatural forces are associated with Him. The truth about God lies within each religion, but each one's concept of Him is different. Religion started from a belief about the unseen things that cause good and horrific events to happen to people. Each religion's fundamentals reside in its truths about life here on earth or life after death. The three elements that made

up religion first start with faith. A religion consists of beliefs, rituals, and ethics. Ideas that form religions are the most important because they give rise to and shape the ethics and the traditions of that faith. The Bible affirms in I Corinthians where Paul shouts, that religion is the substance of things hoped for and the evidence of things unseen.

What is Theology? Theology gives meaning to religion and Mysticism (spiritualism). It researches to clarify the substances used to define the terminology to define the words used to describe both. On the other hand, Philosophy is a pursuit of wisdom. It represented the "driving passion of knowing and understanding." (Morris 1999) The assumption that individual wishes to know why must seek to understand the insight of living. One classification that falls under the discipline of philosophy is ethics. Ethics fit into the disciples of life: philosophy, theology, psychology, and sociology.

THE LAW OF GOD: The Law of God is a promise of the results of humankind's behaviors. The Law of God consists of the Ten Commandments, but there are other types of laws. God instills His Commandments to allow people to see the results of sins and teach them not to sin against Him or themselves. People impelled are to disregard the "thou should not" to choose what is wrong over what is right according to the context of God's codes or Laws.

Religious Philosophers. The movie The Cider House illustrates real-life events that can happen in a person's life. The story centered on the father impregnating his daughter, and the daughter has to choose to keep the child or take the child's life and her father's. The problem and morality of the story are desire and intention.

The choice of living consists of good times or bad ones. Christianity encouraged people to live for today and put aside the desires of the flesh, and if a man desires a woman, he should marry her. The story The Cider House Rules sees happiness happening when life is good, and no problems exist, but unhappiness happens when life is confronted with pain and unsafe pleasure, which can turn into sorrow.

No one is perfect, and all humanity makes mistakes, whether knowing or unknowing. Therefore, they cannot say the problem is a problem when a person knows, or the problem is not a problem when the person does not know, but the problem exists because of choice. Choices can result in power over people, or they can empower others. The story tells of unethical decisions that affect all lives badly.

The Influencing Powers: The book centered on how humanity makes choices to respect no matter the authority. Living in a capitalistic society, man can find it hard to live a moral and righteous lifestyle when unethical life living is practiced in its system. The aim is for man to make ethical choices when living in a society built on the monetary and material gain by any means necessary.

AUGUSTINE OF HIPPOS

What is Sin in the mind of humankind?

 Augustine examined man's mental movements under his design away from religious beliefs' guides to understand the differences between religious beliefs and humanism assurance. He thought a comparison of the two would reveal the reality of religion. Most religions speak in terms of discipline to be more like God, to be able to serve Him, and to be able to come into His presence.

Even though St Augustine (354–430) the father of Western Christianity, believed that sin originates within the individual rather than from the devil's influence. Although his theory appears faulty, the Psalm states that Humankind is shaped in iniquity and conceived in sin in the womb. Still, I do not think it is saying that sin created inequity and corruption but originated within the human body. There is a difference in the understanding, of the account in Genesis when Satan told the woman to disobey God, she would be like God knowing good and evil if she ate the fruit. The act of obeying Satan is the act of sin.

NO GOD

The Theories of non-faith in God are many, but atheism, secularism, humanism, utilitarianism, and" are discussed terms. Their faith in living life tells them they do not have any obligations to God, and they do not have to give an account of the way they live their lives. They are free to do whatever they deem to make them happy, just as long as their actions do not harm another.

Why leave out God in life living to disobey the Laws of God? The Laws of God appeal to humanity's nature and intelligence. If humanity acts against them, their human nature will tell them, and it reminds them what is right or wrong so they cannot ignore their inner soul and intellect. The world sees their actions against God and nature. They do not give Him the glory, not honoring the biblical way of life. They want to live a life of pleasure, not a good one because all the Law of God makes humanity wish to live a good life.

Going against God's will: People see Him, they relate to Him, and they experience God in their everyday life living. The experience of God is according to their faith. Theology teaches about God, but philosophy is deism, a form of monotheism, not a religion but a philosophical idea. The belief sits on the foundation of one God exists, but He does not intervene in the world or interfere with human life and the universe's laws. It posits a non-interfering creator who permits the universe to run itself according to the laws of nature.

Deism derives God's existence and nature from reason and personal experience, rather than relying on revelation in sacred scriptures (which deists see as interpretations made by other humans and not as an authoritative source) or on the proof of others. The direct contrast to Fideism (the view that religious belief depends on faith or revelation rather than reason). The type of sense of deists is a belief, not a religion.

They reject supernatural events such as prophecy, miracles, the divinity of Jesus, and the Trinity's Christian concept. Faith is regarded as a "natural religion as contrasted with one revealed by a God or artificially created by humans." God is an entity in human form. Humanity cannot access God through an organized religion or set of rituals, sacraments, or other practices. They believe God has not selected a chosen people (e.g., Jews or Christians) to be the recipients of any special revelation or gifts. They say God has left his creation behind. Thus, prayer makes no sense, except to express appreciation to God for his works.

Others who fall under the concept of theology leave out small identities of God. First, the word Thesis means belief in one God as creator and ruler of all things, but without evolution. Theists affirmed that an entirely conscious understanding of being, or mind, existing from eternity is the cause of all other things. On the other hand, deism means belief in the existence of a supreme being, specifically of a creator who does not intervene in the universe.

The term was used chiefly during the "intellectual movement of the 17th and 18th centuries" that accepted the existence of a creator based on reason but rejected belief in a supernatural deity who interacts with humankind. Deism is different from Christian deism. Deism is opposed to the doctrine of predestination in which everything that happens is according to the will of God, but instead, tends to believe in the concept of free will. Most of the United States ancestors who wrote the constitution's religious faith were of Christian deism. [4]

Another matter that relates to the belief in God is materialism. Materialism considers material possessions and physical comfort more important than spiritual values. The "ideology of materialism" is an incredibly pervasive philosophy that asserts that nothing exists beyond the material universe, which is composed of matter and energy (with matter and energy, of course, related as described by the work of Albert Einstein, who was not necessarily a materialist). Materialism is the doctrine that nothing exists except matter and its movements and modifications. (5)

Theory of Humanism

Humanity First: Humanism is a philosophical and ethical stance that emphasizes human beings' values, individuality, and collectively, and prefers critical thinking and evidence (rationalism and empiricism) and, between them, set the boundaries of its various in humanisms.

People are motivated to seek a life of goodness and happiness. Philosophers suggest several different schemes to promote people's desire to be better than okay or live safe, among others. Philosophers believe there has to be a philosophical account of morality in people's lives. The problem with all this is the influence to choose. The choice among ethical behavior theories is a difficult one.

Secularism is an irreligion doctrine. Its baseline is not immorality but a shift in the conception of moral powers and moral ends. Secularism is the doctrine that ethics is based solely on humanity's well-being in the spirit of life, to the exclusion of all matters drawn from the belief in God. They say Unitarianism stands with morality rules based solely on humankind's well-being in the present life but not passed on to live in the afterlife; the marginalization of all consideration is drawn from belief in God now and in a future life or even after death. (4 Span; pg. 12)

The secular spirit moves against religions' operations with little self-reliance -reliance only to surrender individual integrity, not to God but also to humanity and social pressers. Faith is the surrender of humanity's life to God and the commitment of life's goods to God's will to honor God's plan, activities, and cause of the righteousness of Church order in communities. The call for a corollary of non-worship to God is centered on the allure and the ultimate objective of secularism. Secularism, many forces in the current life, have affected or blunted man's sense of his dependency to be dependent on God's Word. (4 Pg. 12 Spain)

Secular Humanism

Everybody has Rights: The theory of utilitarianism trusts the actions of usefulness or unity. Utilitarianism is a moral theory that advocates actions that promote overall happiness or pleasure and reject actions that cause unhappiness. Philosophers of this theory say that in producing fun, enjoyment, convenience, or other desirable human advantages, the right story will have the most outstanding quality of positive states. Utilitarianism believes that morality aims to make life better by increasing the number of good things (such as pleasure and happiness) and decreasing the number of terrible things (such as pain and unhappiness). They reject moral codes or systems that consist of commands or taboos based on customs, traditions, or orders given by leaders or supernatural beings. Instead, it is useful to think that what makes morality valid or justifiable is its positive contribution to human (and non-human) beings.

All six-influence theories of behavior give ideas. The theory is based on the excellent conduct of humanity, even though ethical attributes are not present. The bottom line is humankind's reasonability to determine what is right and what is wrong or what is moral and what is not ethical as human beings' nature supersedes all thought or influences. Character displays how humanity is proposed to live among each other, not as animals in the animal kingdom but as intelligent human beings.

Secular Humanitarians

Secular humanism is a philosophy or life stance that embraces human reason. Secular ethics and philosophical naturalism while specifically rejecting religious dogma, supernaturalism, and superstition based on morality and decision-making. Secular humanism posits that human beings can be ethical and moral without religion or belief in a deity. However, it does not assume that humans are either inherently good or evil or present humans as superior to nature. Instead, the humanist life stance emphasizes humanity's responsibility and the ethical consequences of human decisions.

Cited from the Xavier Comte writer who formulated the doctrine of positivism.

Many secular humanists derive their moral codes from a philosophy of utilitarianism, ethical naturalism, or evolutionary ethics. Some advocate the science of morality. Psychology has to do with the study of behavior and the mind of a human, or the scientific study of the human mind and its functions, especially those affecting behavior in a given context, such as the mental and emotional factors governing a situation or activity. There are distinct types of psychology, such as cognitive, forensic, social, and developmental psychology, but all have one purpose, to study the mind and its outputs.

Unitarianism

Utilitarianism sees equality with all human beings. They based their ethical theories on "maximizing happiness and well-being for all affected individuals." The basic idea behind utilitarianism thought is "maximize utility. Often defined in terms of well-being or related concepts." Jeremy Bentham, the founder of utilitarianism, described utility as "that property in any object, whereby it tends to produce benefit, advantage, pleasure, good, or happiness or prevent the happening of mischief, pain, evil, or unhappiness to the party who's considered interest."

Spiritualism

Therefore, the definition of spiritualism embraces a vast array of highly diversified philosophical views. In philosophy, spiritualism represents many characteristics of any thought system that "affirms the existence of immaterial reality imperceptible to the senses." So defined, spiritualism embraces a vast array of highly diversified philosophical views. Most patently, it applies to any philosophy accepting the notion of an infinite, "personal God, the immortality of the soul, or the immateriality of the intellect and will." Less obviously, it includes belief in such "ideas as finite cosmic forces or a universal mind provided that they transcend the limits of gross materialistic interpretation." Spiritualism affirms nothing about the matter, the nature of a supreme being or a universal force, or the precise nature of spiritual reality itself.

Notes: https://www.britannica.com/topic/spiritualism-philosophy

REFERENCES

1. Smith, Huston. *World's Religions*, HarperCollins Publications: New York, NY, 1994
2. Esposito, John L., Fasching, Darrell J., and Lewis, Todd. World Religions today, Oxford University Press: New York, NY, 2009
3. Richard, Spann J. The Christian Faith and Secularism, New York, NY: Abingdon-Cokesbury Press,
4. Johnston, Jerry. Apostasy Now, Overland Park, Kansas: Jerry Johnston Publishing

Notes: Smith, Huston. New York, NY: HarperCollins Publishers, 1994

"The Author's Notes and the Bookends"

www.ingramcontent.com/pod-product-compliance
Lightning Source LLC
Chambersburg PA
CBHW071739120626

46550CB00002B/590